How Did Davy Die?
And Why Do We Care So Much?

Number Thirty-Six
Elma Dill Russell Spencer Series
in the West and Southwest

How Did Davy Die?
And Why Do We Care
So Much?

DAN KILGORE AND JAMES E. CRISP

Commemorative Edition, Enlarged

Texas A&M University Press
College Station

The paper used in this book
meets the minimum requirements
of the American National Standard for Permanence
of Paper for Printed Library Materials, Z39.48-1984.
Binding materials have been chosen for durability.

LIBRARY OF CONGRESS CATALOGING-IN-PUBLICATION DATA

Kilgore, Dan, 1921–1995.
How did Davy die? And why do we care so much? / Dan Kilgore and
James E. Crisp. — Commemorative ed., enl.
p. cm. — (Elma Dill Russell Spencer series in the West and Southwest ;
no. 36)
"First chapter of publication consists of complete text and notes of original
edition. Second chapter is all new material and notes."
—ECIP data view comments.
Portion comprising original text first published in 1978 under the title:
How did Davy die?
ISBN-13: 978-1-60344-194-0 (cloth : alk. paper)
ISBN-10: 1-60344-194-8 (cloth : alk. paper)
1. Crockett, Davy, 1786-1836.   2. Crockett, Davy, 1786-1836—Death
and burial.   3. Alamo (San Antonio, Tex.)—Siege, 1836.   4. Texas—
Historiography.   5. Kilgore, Dan, 1921–1995—Influence.   6. Kilgore,
Dan, 1921–1995. How did Davy die?   I. Crisp, James E., 1946–
II. Kilgore, Dan, 1921–1995. How did Davy die?   III. Title.   IV. Series:
Elma Dill Russell Spencer series in the West and Southwest ; no. 36.
F436.C95D36   2010
976.8'04092—dc22
2009036880

Engraving on p. 8 courtesy Kelsey Americana Collection,
Cushing Memorial Library and Archives, Texas A&M University.
Engraving on p. 50 courtesy Texas Collection,
Cushing Memorial Library and Archives, Texas A&M University

Acknowledgments

THIS ESSAY originated as the presidential address to the Texas State Historical Association on March 4, 1977. Many friends assisted in searching for the sources used in the original paper and in this expanded and revised version. My special thanks and gratitude go to the following people who sought out obscure references and searched for sources that never materialized: J. Richard Abell, Lucile Boykin, Doug Ferrier, Llerena Friend, Johnny and Maureen Jenkins, Chester V. Kielman and his accommodating staff at Barker Texas History Center, Christopher La Plante, Archie P. McDonald, Catherine McDowell, Malcolm D. and Margaret McLean, Robert A. Nesbitt, Rhoda Poenisch, James B. Stewart, Margaret Turner, Fred White, Sr., Dorman Winfrey, John Young, and my wife, Carol.

DAN KILGORE

How Did Davy Die?

DAN KILGORE

Fall of the Alamo---Death of Crockett.

How Did Davy Die?

THE GOOD LORD generously endowed David Crockett with those qualities the backwoods required: rugged strength, unusual perseverance, extraordinary courage, and fierce determination. Crockett capitalized on those gifts and employed his wit, imagination, and charm to gain national prominence as the central character of many a tall tale and to earn renown in his own time as one of America's greatest folk heroes. Yet Crockett's death at the Alamo in 1836 came as a tragic finale to a life that was essentially a failure in achievement of worldly goals. He died a poor man with an undistinguished record as a congressman.

The simplicities of backwoods life did not prepare him for the intricacies of politics in Washington. He won three congressional terms, but he failed consistently in his main political goal: to win passage of the Tennessee Vacant Land Bill. His bill would have granted frontiersmen the right to buy their homesteads at low cost and on credit. It was a bill designed for his "squatter constituency," whom he considered the nation's advance guard.

Throughout Crockett's rise to prominence as a national figure, political enemies defeated him at every turn, although both major parties used him as a symbol at various times and employed the national press to establish that symbol. During the years that Crockett supported Andrew Jackson, the Democratic press polished Crockett's image with little regard for the real man. At the same time, Whig newspapers, with just as little respect for fact, tried to laugh him out of Congress. After his opposition to Jackson's Indian Removal Bill brought about his defeat for reelection in 1831, he bitterly opposed Jackson for the rest of his life. As a result, when Crockett returned to Congress in 1833, the Democratic papers reversed their position and echoed the old Whig line against him. At that same time, the Whigs adopted and even refined the earlier image of the frontier hero started by the Democrats.

In 1835 Crockett's passionate opposition to Jackson resulted in a particularly bitter defeat for him in his try for reelection to Congress. Loss of office and of the attendant public attention cut deeply. Within weeks Crockett left Tennessee and headed for Texas.[1]

Crockett's last extant letter discloses that he and

[1] James Atkins Shackford, *David Crockett: The Man and the Legend* (Chapel Hill, N.C., 1956), pp. 191, 210–212, 221, 238–239, 241–245.

his party departed Tennessee in November, 1835, to explore a new country for his next move west. This was his stated purpose—and not "to fight for his rights" or even for Texas independence. He examined the country along the Red River in Texas and called it the garden spot of the world. He hoped to live there—hoped to be appointed land agent to settle the area and then to acquire the fortune that had always eluded him. When his funds ran short, he sold an engraved gold presentation watch for a cheaper timepiece and thirty dollars.

After inspecting the Red River lands, Crockett and his men made a side trip to hunt buffalo that were moving south in their annual migration.[2] By mid-January, 1836, Crockett was in San Augustine, where he signed an oath of allegiance to Texas so that he could vote and seek election to the approaching constitutional convention. He left San Augustine with the apparent intention of resuming his political career in Texas, but at that point the real David Crockett fades almost completely into myth and legend. No further written word from him survives to explain why he failed to campaign for a seat in the constitutional convention. His biographer, James Shackford, believed that Crockett's hatred for Jackson drove him instead to the Alamo.

[2] Ibid., pp. 214–216; John H. Jenkins (ed.), *The General's Tight Pants: Edward Warren's Texas Tour of 1836* (Austin, 1976).

In early 1836 two political groups and two governments, the Consultation Convention and the General Council, contended for political and military control of the budding Republic of Texas. The division, the same quarrel that drove Crockett from Tennessee, lay between pro-Jackson and anti-Jackson forces. Sam Houston, considered to be Jackson's personal representative, served as commander in chief under the Consultation Convention, but Houston could not exercise control over the command at the Alamo. Shackford believed that Crockett joined the Alamo defenders to demonstrate further opposition to the Jackson forces that had defeated him in Tennessee and not with any idea of dying for the liberty of Texas.

Crockett passed on through the capital at Washington-on-the-Brazos and entered San Antonio before February 11. He had never been known to run out on a fight, and once he arrived at the Alamo, he never left.[3] Tales of his prowess emanated from frontier observers and spread across Texas and then throughout the United States in a blend of fact and folklore.

William B. Travis mentioned in a letter dated February 25, 1836, that during the initial bombardment of the Alamo, "The Hon. David Crockett was seen at all points, animating the men to do their duty." A northern newspaper later quoted a Natchitoches man as

[3] Shackford, *David Crockett*, pp. 216–224.

saying Crockett's "unerring rifle . . . marked down" five Mexican soldiers as each stepped forward to fire a cannon planted within gunshot of the fort. A letter dated March 2 at Goliad told how Crockett probably "grinned off" the attackers. Another on March 10 said (in original spelling), "Davy Crockett and James Bowy are fighting at San Antone like tigers."[4]

After the fall of the Alamo, as a survivor of Fannin's Goliad command wrote, it was told that Crockett killed the first Mexican soldier at a distance of two hundred yards. He and Lieutenant Dickenson then allegedly burned several houses which were sheltering the enemy from Texas artillery. The same writer added, ". . . it is said and generally believed in Texas of Col. Crockett, that when Gen. Santa Anna was surveying the Alamo for the purpose of informing himself of the best method of arranging an attack, he [Crockett] made so good a shot at him as to come near taking his life, which so much enraged the General, that he resolved to storm the fort the next day and he kept his resolution."[5]

Crockett's heroism seemed to expand in direct proportion to the distance news about him had to travel. A resolution adopted after the Alamo's fall, at

[4] John H. Jenkins (ed.), *The Papers of the Texas Revolution, 1835–1836*, 10 vols. (Austin, 1973), IV, 433, 487; V, 45; *The Metropolitan* (Georgetown and Washington, D.C.), July 13, 1836.

[5] Jenkins, *Papers of the Texas Revolution*, IX, 183, 223.

a meeting in Nacogdoches on March 26, declared that "David Crockett (now rendered immortal in Glory) had fortified himself with sixteen guns well charged, and a monument of slain foes encompasses his lifeless body." A letter written from San Augustine on March 29 declared, "The Honorable David Crockett . . . was found dead with about 20 of the enemy with him and his rifle was broken to pieces it is supposed that he killed at least 20 or 30 himself."[6]

Various rumors that Crockett survived the assault on the Alamo arose almost simultaneously with his death, but no real evidence has turned up to suggest that he survived the battle. Valid documentation survives, however, to support the view that he did not fall surrounded by mounds of the slain enemy, but that he either surrendered or was captured near the end of the assault and was immediately killed by Santa Anna's order. Published references indicating that Crockett surrendered have drawn loud protests from both the press and an irate public throughout the years. Most recently *Texas Monthly* bestowed one of its 1975 uncoveted "Bum Steer" awards on what that magazine described as "A recent translation of a Mexican officer's diary which revealed that Davy Crockett surrendered at the Alamo, and was executed some time after the battle."[7]

[6] Ibid., V, 224; IX, 160.
[7] *Texas Monthly*, February, 1976, p. 79.

Lieutenant José Enrique de la Peña, who was one of Santa Anna's officers, wrote the diary during the Mexican army's Texas campaign in 1836. He did not, however, say that Crockett surrendered. Texas A&M University Press published the diary, translated from the Spanish by Carmen Perry, in October, 1975, under the title *With Santa Anna in Texas: A Personal Narrative of the Revolution.* Throughout his daily record, de la Peña was strongly critical of his general's conduct of the war against Texas. His single paragraph describing Crockett's capture and death, however, caught the eye and roused the ire of several Texas publications. Carmen Perry drew some of the barbs, although her part consisted only of rendering into English what de la Peña had written in his native language.

The diary's author participated in the storming of the Alamo on March 6, 1836, witnessed the entire battle, and recorded his observations soon afterward. His diary was first published in Mexico in 1955 in the original Spanish.

According to de la Peña, the desperate fighting ended shortly after six o'clock in the morning. Santa Anna then entered the Alamo fortifications to survey the gruesome scene and to laud his crippled battalions. De la Peña wrote:

Shortly before Santa Anna's speech, an unpleasant episode had taken place, which . . . was looked upon as base murder.

15

. . . Some seven men had survived the general carnage and, under the protection of General Castrillón, they were brought before Santa Anna. Among them . . . was the naturalist David Crockett, well known in North America for his unusual adventures. . . . Santa Anna answered Castrillón's intervention in Crockett's behalf with a gesture of indignation and, addressing himself to . . . the troops closest to him, ordered his execution. The commanders and officers were outraged at this action and did not support the order . . . ; but several officers who were around the president and who, perhaps, had not been present during the moment of danger . . . thrust themselves forward, . . . and with swords in hand, fell upon these unfortunate, defenseless men just as a tiger leaps upon his prey. Though tortured before they were killed, these unfortunates died without complaining and without humiliating themselves before their torturers.[8]

Six other Mexican soldiers support de la Peña's testimony that Crockett was one of several Texans who was captured or who surrendered and then was killed. Besides these seven soldiers, other sources that do not mention Crockett by name say that from five to seven Alamo defenders were taken alive, marched before Santa Anna, and executed by his order.

The most prestigious Mexican source is Ramón Martínez Caro, Santa Anna's personal secretary, who

[8] José Enrique de la Peña, *With Santa Anna in Texas: A Personal Narrative of the Revolution*, trans. and ed. Carmen Perry (College Station, Tex., 1975), pp. 52–53; J. Sanchez Garza (ed.), *La Rebelion de Texas: Manuscrito inedito de 1836, por un oficial de Santa Anna* (Mexico City, 1955), p. 70.

reported in his "True Account" that ". . . five men . . . hid themselves, and when the action was over, General Castrillón found them and brought them into the presence of Santa Anna, who, for a moment angrily reprimanded the said general, and then turned his back; at which act the soldiers already lined up, charged the prisoners and killed them."[9]

Martínez Caro's statement was largely corroborated by the first word of the fall of the Alamo delivered to General Sam Houston. On the day of the battle two ranchers living near present Floresville gathered as much information as possible from San Antonio and hurried to tell General Houston, then at Gonzales. Houston included the information in a letter written March 11 to James W. Fannin, commander at Goliad. "After the fort was carried, seven men surrendered and called for Santa Anna and quarter," Houston wrote. "They were murdered by his order."[10] Although Martínez Caro and Houston differed on the number of men involved, they agreed on basic facts.

Travelers from Texas arriving in New Orleans on March 27, 1836, three weeks after the assault, brought

[9] Carlos E. Castañeda (ed.), *The Mexican Side of the Texas Revolution* (Dallas, 1928), pp. 103–104.

[10] Jenkins, *Papers of the Texas Revolution*, V, 45–49, 52–54, 69–71; Amelia W. Williams and Eugene C. Barker (eds.), *The Writings of Sam Houston, 1813–1836*, 8 vols. (Austin, 1938), I, 362–365.

the first news of the battle. The *New Orleans Post-Union* reported that "Crockett and others had tried to surrender 'but were told there was no mercy for them.' "[11] Northern newspapers reprinted this news, which was probably the first word received throughout the United States of the fall of the Alamo and of the death of David Crockett.

Within months after the battle this account of the capture and execution of Crockett appeared in two different books published in the United States. Mary Austin Holley used the *Post-Union's* very words regarding the denial of mercy in her book *Texas*, released in July, 1836. "A desperate contest ensued," she wrote of the battle, "in which prodigies of valor were wrought by this Spartan band." She said that Crockett and six others "cried for quarter, but were told there was no mercy for them. . . . When their demand for quarter was refused, they continued fighting until all were butchered."[12]

The second book, also published during the summer of 1836, sought to establish a hero of gigantic proportions. Its title was *Col. Crockett's Exploits and Adventures in Texas, Written by Himself*. This apocry-

[11] Walter Lord, *A Time to Stand* (New York, 1961), p. 207.

[12] Mrs. Mary Austin Holley, *Texas* (Lexington, Ky., 1836), pp. 353–354; Mattie Austin Hatcher, *Letters of an Early American Traveller; Mary Austin Holley, Her Life and Works, 1784–1846* (Dallas, 1933), p. 61.

phal but best-selling "autobiography" opened the floodgates of Crockett mythology, and although patently spurious, it has remained in print in many editions through most of the years since.

While scholars have dismissed the book's version of Crockett's death as pure fiction, the "narrative" depicting the scene was largely "brought down . . . by an eye-witness," as stated on the book's title page. The lurid description of the hero's final moments, created from a montage of contemporary news clippings, primarily was extracted verbatim from the previously published statement of a Mexican prisoner who was an eyewitness.

Specific words attributed to the eyewitness appear in italics in the quotation below taken from *Exploits and Adventures*. As dawn approached, only six Alamo defenders were found alive. Crockett stood alone, a frightful gash across his forehead, in an angle of the fort, with the barrel of his shattered rifle in his right hand and with a Bowie knife, dripping blood, in his left. Some twenty dead or dying Mexicans lay around him.

[The defenders] *were instantly surrounded and ordered, by General Castrillon, to surrender,* which they did, *under a promise of his protection, finding* that *resistance any longer* would be *madness. . . .*

General *Castrillon was brave and not cruel, and disposed to save* the prisoners. *He marched them up to that part*

19

of the fort where stood Santa Anna and his *murderous crew. The steady, fearless step, and undaunted tread* of Colonel Crockett in this occasion, *together with the bold demeanor* of the *hardy veteran,* had a *powerful effect* on all present. *Nothing daunted, he marched up boldly in front of Santa Anna,* and *looked him* sternly *in the face, while Castrillon addressed "his excellency,"—"Sir, here are six prisoners I have taken alive; how shall I dispose of them?" Santa Anna looked at Castrillon fiercely, flew into a violent rage, and replied, "Have I not told you before how to dispose of them? Why do you bring them to me?" At the same time his brave officers plunged their swords into the bosoms of their defenceless prisoners.*

Colonel Crockett, seeing the act of treachery, instantly sprang like a tiger at the ruffian chief, but before he could reach him a dozen swords were sheathed in his indomitable heart; and he fell, and died without a groan, a frown on his brow, and a smile of scorn and defiance on his lips. *Castrillon rushed from the scene, apparently horror-struck, sought his quarters, and did not leave them for several days, and hardly spoke to Santa Anna after.*[13]

The lines italicized above were taken from a letter written from Galveston Bay on June 9, 1836, by a correspondent of the *New York Courier and Enquirer* following an interview with an unidentified Mexican prisoner (who sounded suspiciously like Ramón Martínez Caro to historian Walter Lord) among Santa Anna's troops who had been captured at San Jacinto and who

[13] *Col. Crockett's Exploits and Adventures in Texas, Written by Himself* (Philadelphia, 1836), pp. 203–205.

were then being held on Galveston Island. After the appearance in the New York newspaper of this particular account, it was reprinted—a common journalistic practice of the time—in other publications, including the *Frankfort* (Kentucky) *Commonwealth*.[14]

More than a century later the story of Crockett's death as presented in *Exploits and Adventures* provoked what might be called the opening shot in the modern battle over the circumstances of Crockett's death. The October, 1943, issue of *Southwestern Historical Quarterly* carried a reader's inquiry about the source of a statement that Crockett "was one of the six survivors who surrendered to Santa Anna and were shot down by his orders. . . ." That statement had appeared in the *Biographical Directory of the American Congresses, 1774–1927*, and, in similar context, in the *Columbia Encyclopedia*. The editor of the quarterly did not provide an answer about the source, but he felt (as he later disclosed) that the stories of the surrender were taken from the "'spurious" ending of *Exploits and Adventures*. The editor replied simply but wrathfully,

[14] *Frankfort* (Kentucky) *Commonwealth*, July 27, 1836; Lord, *A Time to Stand*, pp. 206–207. The phrases "in an angle," "lying pell-mell," and "a frown on his brow, a smile of scorn upon his lips" appear in an article reprinted in *The Metropolitan* (Georgetown and Washington, D.C.), May 11, 1836. Andrew Briscoe reported that Crockett fell fighting "like a tiger" in the *Louisiana Advertiser*, March 28, 1836, as reprinted in the *Broome Republican* (Binghamton, N.Y.), April 21, 1836.

"The people of Tennessee and Texas will need more authority than *The Congressional Directory* and a New York publication to be convinced that David Crockett surrendered."[15] Possibly because of the editor's rebuke, both publications dropped references in later editions to the surrender.

Although sources now available do not offer absolute proof that Crockett actually surrendered or was captured, a preponderance of evidence supports the unidentified prisoner's story retold in *Exploits and Adventures*. Neither of the two known adult Texan survivors, Mrs. Dickenson and the slave Joe, saw Crockett die. Since Santa Anna and his men were the only others present, any evidence must come from them. Besides the unknown prisoner and de la Peña, four officers and a sergeant—all of whom participated in the assault and observed the final tragedy—specifically identified Crockett as one of the captives.[16] Statements from these seven Mexican soldiers were mutually corroborative and were recorded independently under

[15] H. Bailey Carroll, "Texas Collection," *Southwestern Historical Quarterly* 47: 178; H. Bailey Carroll, "David Crockett," in *Heroes of Texas* (Waco, 1964), p. 66; Thomas Lawrence Conelly (ed.); "Did David Crockett Surrender at the Alamo? A Contemporary Letter," *Journal of Southern History* 26: 368.

[16] Richard G. Santos, *Santa Anna's Campaign against Texas, 1835–1836: Featuring the Field Commands Issued to Major General Vicente Filisola* (Waco, 1968), pp. 76 n. 73, 84.

widely differing circumstances. Their accounts have come to light over a long period of time, several having surfaced only recently. Any one of them, standing alone, could be subject to question, but considered as a whole, the statements provide stronger documentation than can be claimed for any other incident during the battle.

The first known version by a participant to be published in permanent form appeared in the 1859 *Texas Almanac* in an article by Dr. D. N. Labadie, who had treated many wounded Mexicans after the Battle of San Jacinto. Only four or five days after Santa Anna's defeat, Dr. Labadie dressed the wounded hip of Colonel Fernando Urissa, Santa Anna's aide, who told the doctor: "I observed Castrion [*sic*] coming out of one of the quarters, leading a venerable looking old man by the hand; he [the old man] was tall, his face was red, and stooped forward as he walked." Urissa told Labadie he heard Mexicans call the man "Coket." Castrillón asked his commander to spare the "venerable old man," but Santa Anna berated him for disobeying orders to take no prisoners. Then the general ordered nearby soldiers to shoot the captive. Urissa convinced Labadie he was telling the truth about Crockett's fate.[17]

[17] James M. Day (comp.), *The Texas Almanac, 1857–1873: A Compendium of Texas History* (Waco, 1967), p. 174.

The most bizarre account of Crockett's death by a participant at the Alamo was related to Reuben M. Potter and later to John S. Ford, both important writers of Texas history. The eyewitness was Sergeant Francisco Becerra, who took upon himself a major role in the incident. Ford wrote down the sergeant's story in 1875, and it apparently appeared in print soon thereafter to stir angry criticism before fading into obscurity. In 1957 the story was extracted from Ford's manuscript memoirs and reappeared in a booklet published in Brownsville.[18] Although Sergeant Becerra is probably the least reliable Alamo eyewitness, he may be the unacknowledged source of more details written about the assault than any other participant.

After his capture at the Battle of San Jacinto, Becerra remained in Texas the rest of his life. He worked for several well-known Texans, including Mirabeau B. Lamar and Reuben M. Potter. Becerra eventually settled in Brownsville, where in 1875 Ford recorded his recollections of Santa Anna's campaign. His version of Crockett's death aroused as much indignation as did the version in de la Peña's diary published one hundred years later.

[18] José Tomás Canales (ed.), *Bits of Texas History in the Melting Pot of America: Part II, Native Latin American Contributions to Colonization and Independence of Texas* (Brownsville, 1957), pp. 19–20.

Becerra told Ford he shot the ailing Bowie in his bed after seeing Bowie kill two other Mexican soldiers with two pistols. After dispatching the Texas hero, Becerra said, he entered another room and found Travis sitting on the floor. Becerra told Ford he saw Travis offer a bugler a roll of bank bills in exchange for his life.

The bugler was dividing the money with him, Becerra said, when he saw Crockett arise from the floor where he had been lying, apparently exhausted, after the hard fight. At that moment Cos and three other generals entered the room.

As soon as Gen. Cos saw the gentleman who spoke Spanish, he rushed to him, and embraced him. He told the other generals it was Travis; that on a former occasion he had treated him like a brother, had loaned him money, etc. He also said the other man was Col. Crockett. He entreated the other generals to go with him to Gen. Santa Anna, and join with him in a request to save the lives of the two Texans. The bugler and myself followed them. They encountered the Commander-in-Chief in the court yard, with Gen. Castrillon. Gen. Cos said to him: "Mr. President, you have here two prisoners—in the name of the Republic of Mexico, I supplicate you to guarantee the lives of both." Santa Anna was very much enraged. He said: "Gentlemen generals, my order was to kill every man in the Alamo." He turned and said: "Soldiers, kill them." . . . soldiers standing around opened fire. A shot struck Travis in the back. He then stood erect, folded his arms, and looked calmly, unflinchingly, upon his assailants. He was finally killed by a ball passing through his neck. Crockett stood in a similar position. They died undaunted like heroes.[19]

Twenty years after talking with Becerra, Ford quoted him at great length on operations of the Mexican army in *Origin and Fall of the Alamo,* published in 1895. Ford chose not to use Becerra's version of Crockett's death in that work. The furor that had resulted from the earlier publication of the details apparently caused him to omit them. He wrote instead, "Sergeant Becerra was of opinion that the last two men killed were Travis and Col. Crockett, though he admitted he did not know them personally, and might be mistaken as to their identity."[20]

The appearance of the sergeant's version in print in the 1870's had drawn the fire of serious historians. In 1878 a *New York World* correspondent followed Ford's rendition of Becerra's tale closely, at times verbatim, in an article entitled "Storming of the Alamo." Although the correspondent attributed his "peculiar version of the story affecting the death of Travis and Crockett" to a soldier named "Buerra," the source certainly was Becerra.[21] The same version of the deaths

[19] Ibid; "A Mexican Sergeant's Recollections of the Alamo and San Jacinto," *Texas Mute Ranger,* April, 1882, pp. 169–172.

[20] John S. Ford, *Origin and Fall of the Alamo, March 6, 1836* (San Antonio, 1895), p. 21.

[21] *Albert Hanford's Texas State Register for 1878* (Galveston, 1878), p. 30.

of Travis and Crockett (but attributed only to "a Mexican soldier") appeared again in a historical section of an 1882 San Antonio guidebook.[22] These two publications caught the attention of historian Hubert Howe Bancroft, who denounced them. Bancroft said the stories that Travis "as well as Crockett was one of the captives put to death, are utterly unworthy of credence."[23]

Becerra's tale also eventually aroused the wrath of his former employer, historian Reuben M. Potter, who had previously praised the sergeant in his own Alamo narrative. Potter had criticized the surrender story on several other occasions through the years before encountering, in print, Becerra's version of the surrender.

In January, 1880, Potter responded to an article, "The Massacre of the Alamo," published in his hometown newspaper. He called the article a calumny against the hero and stoutly maintained that "David Crockett never surrendered to bear or tiger, Indian or Mexican."[24]

An 1883 article in the *Magazine of American History* recounting Crockett's surrender as told in *Exploits and Adventures* drew Potter's expanded criticism. Pot-

[22] Stephen Gould, *The Alamo City Guide, San Antonio, Texas* (San Antonio, 1882), p. 21.

[23] Hubert Howe Bancroft, *History of the North Mexican States and Texas*, 2 vols. (San Francisco, 1889), II, 211.

[24] Clipping from *The Independent Hour*, Woodbridge (?), January 26, 1880, Reuben M. Potter scrapbook, pp. 278–279, University of Texas Archives, Austin.

ter said he considered the defense of the Alamo one of the most heroic events in our history. He stated his conviction that every man in the garrison, including Crockett, fell fighting at his post—with the exception of "a few skulkers." Even these skulkers did not surrender, he said, but were dragged from their hiding place and executed.[25]

Three years later Becerra's elaborated story about Crockett's surrender appeared in the June, 1886, edition of *Magazine of American History* as "derived from a Mexican soldier in the army of Santa Anna." Potter fired off a reiteration of his position that the Alamo's defense was one of the most heroic events in history. Then he theorized, "In a fight . . . [when the hopelessly outnumbered] know they have all got to die, the bravest fall first; and the last reached is certain to be a sneak. Thus it was at the Alamo. Travis and Crockett fell early on the outworks." Potter blasted the tale attributed to the Mexican soldier: "This infamous fiction confounds [Travis and Crockett] with the group of skulkers already referred to, and ought never to have been cited, even as a rumor, in any matter which claims to be historical."[26]

[25] Marcus J. Wright, "Colonel David Crockett, of Tennessee," *Magazine of American History* 10: 489; R. M. Potter, "Colonel David Crockett," *Magazine of American History* 11: 177–178.

[26] G. Norton Galloway, "Sketch of San Antonio: The Fall of the Alamo," *Magazine of American History* 15: 532–533; R. M.

Although Becerra was not named, Potter must have known that his former servant was the source of the scorned account. Potter had used much information given him by Becerra in his study of the fall of the Alamo—an account that a serious student of the battle called the most authoritative source originating from a writer living at the time.[27] After the first publication in 1860 in pamphlet form, Potter's Alamo study gained wider circulation when reprinted in the 1868 *Texas Almanac*. Then it received national distribution in a revised and enlarged version published in the *Magazine of American History* in 1878.

Although Potter did not mention Becerra's tale of the deaths of Bowie, Travis, and Crockett in his Alamo study, he did single out the Mexican as one of "three intelligent sergeants [who provided details], who were men of fair education, and I think truthful." Potter did say that Becerra witnessed Lieutenant Dickenson's leap, saw Bowie's body on the bed, and observed the execution of the men found concealed after the battle.[28] Further, he obviously had relied heavily on Becerra's accounts of the Mexican army's march into Texas, of its

---

Potter, "The Legendary Alamo, "*Magazine of American History* 16: 211–212.

[27] Lon Tinkle, *13 Days to Glory: The Siege of the Alamo* (New York, 1958), p. 248.

[28] R. M. Potter, "The Fall of the Alamo," *Magazine of American History* 2: 19–20.

occupation of San Antonio, and of many incidents during the siege of the Alamo and the final assault.

An examination of Potter's writing shows that he changed his own position on Crockett's death. Originally he had written, "Crockett had taken refuge in a room of the lower barracks near the gate . . . he sallied to meet his fate . . . and was shot down."[29] In the 1878 revision he said, "According to Mr. Ruiz, then the Alcalde of San Antonio, who, after the action, was required to point out the slain leaders to Santa Anna, the body of Crockett was found in the west battery. . . ."[30] Furthermore, it seems apparent that initially Potter was not favorably impressed by Crockett. Potter described another Alamo hero, James Bonham, as a "polished jewel," but he referred to Crockett as a "rough gem" who represented a squatter constituency in Congress.[31] Fifty years after the battle and twenty-five years after the first publication of his study, however, Potter was quite ready to accept the heroic Crockett.

Potter's account of the defense and fall of the Alamo remained as the only major study published until the 1930's. Numerous authors of early Texas histories quoted it entirely or in part and described it as "most complete and reliable" and "most accurate."[32]

[29] Day, *Texas Almanac*, p. 257.
[30] Ibid., p. 357; Potter, "Fall of the Alamo," p. 13.
[31] Potter, "Fall of the Alamo," p. 5.
[32] John Henry Brown, *History of Texas, from 1685 to 1892*,

In 1914 Eugene C. Barker, the distinguished Texas historian, termed it the most thorough study yet made.[33] More recent works on the Alamo, supported by documents not available to Potter, prove the error of some of his conclusions, but they cannot negate his influence on earlier historians.

Nor can Potter be criticized for choosing not to use Becerra's story about the deaths of men enshrined long ago as Texas heroes, although his acceptance of Becerra's word on Mexican army activities establishes the sergeant as the principal source of many details of the siege and assault of the Alamo. When Becerra spoke on army operations, he related facts, most of which could be verified from other sources.

But Becerra's yarn about his Alamo involvement with Bowie, Travis, and Crockett was, and is, hard to believe. The truth may never be known, but the answer could lie in this forgotten man's search for personal glorification or in the telling around campfires of too many tales.

Becerra fought much longer in the service of Texas than of Mexico. According to Ford, Becerra

2 vols. (St. Louis, 1892), I, 569; Dudley G. Wooten (ed.), *A Comprehensive History of Texas, 1685–1897*, 2 vols. (Dallas, 1898), II, 637.

[33] Frank W. Johnson, *A History of Texas and Texans*, ed. Eugene C. Barker and E. W. Winkler, 5 vols. (Chicago, 1914), I, 410.

served in the Indian campaigns of 1839, fought in 1849 along the border under Captain Mirabeau B. Lamar, and later became "a strong supporter of the Southern cause" as a lieutenant in Captain J. F. Parker's company.[34] So much Texas military service would have pitted him against some of the world's best tall tale spinners, and all indications are that he could hold his own. Perhaps Becerra actually came to believe through years of yarn spinning that he had indeed been personally involved with the three Alamo heroes. At least he convinced Ford.

Many years passed before the appearance in print of another account of an eyewitness. In 1836 Dr. George M. Patrick had told a story involving Crockett and General Cos to W. P. Zuber, who included it long afterwards as an appendage to a letter, written in 1904, denying the surrender of any Alamo defenders. The letter was not published until 1939, when it appeared in that year's publication of the Texas Folklore Society, entitled *In the Shadow of History*.

Zuber could be called the greatest Alamo folklorist, because he is the single source for the most dramatic episodes of the gallant defense. Only through Zuber does the world know of Travis's impassioned before-the-battle speech which Zuber literally composed during "a phenomenal refreshment of memory."

[34] "A Mexican Sergeant's Recollections," p. 169.

Only on Zuber's word do we know of Travis's drawing that legendary sword-etched line in the dirt of the Alamo floor. Only Zuber told of the ailing Bowie asking his comrades to lift his cot over the line and of Moses Rose declining to step across, thereby becoming the last man to leave the garrison and escape the slaughter.

Many historians have questioned Zuber's tales, and some have voiced doubt that Rose was ever a member of the Alamo garrison. Zuber devoted much of his later life to writing down, then defending, what his parents had gleaned from Moses Rose while Rose recuperated at the Zuber home during his 1836 flight from the Alamo. Appropriately, Zuber's 1904 letter appeared in the same publication that first offered proof, from testimony entered in the early records of Nacogdoches County, that Rose had been present at the Alamo.

The primary thrust of Zuber's letter published by the Texas Folklore Society was that the tales of the Texans found in hiding after the battle were nothing more than fabrications. After discounting these stories, Zuber recounted what Dr. George M. Patrick told him about the capture of Crockett.

According to Zuber, Dr. Patrick said that he visited General Martín Perfecto de Cos, Santa Anna's brother-in-law, while Cos was being held prisoner after his capture at San Jacinto. Patrick asked the general if he had seen Crockett and if he knew how he had died. Cos answered that he, not Castrillón, had found Crockett, who was well dressed and locked alone in a room in the barracks. Zuber then composed a fanciful entreaty by Crockett, presumably based on what he said Patrick had told him years earlier. Zuber quoted Crockett as explaining that he came to Texas to explore and to become a loyal Mexican citizen, and that he had done no fighting. Following this, Zuber presented a similarly flowery plea by Cos, who had taken Crockett before Santa Anna with the supplication that his brother-in-law spare the distinguished former congressman. Zuber had Santa Anna answering impatiently, "You know your orders," and turning away. Crockett struck at Santa Anna with a dagger, but "was met by a bayonet-thrust by the hand of a soldier through the heart."

Zuber denounced this tale as a gross falsehood because of inaccurate details, which he had provided himself. Yet when he later wrote his memoirs, he gave differing versions of these same details. It appears that Zuber, as he once accused a historian who questioned him, ". . . sometimes relied too much upon his memory in stating historical facts."

Zuber began and ended his letter by stating that not one Texan "escaped or surrendered, or tried to do so; but every man of them died fighting." To admit that any of the brave defenders, particularly Crockett, surrendered or were captured would violate Zuber's basic theme of the Alamo defense as a great heroic epic. Still, Zuber's letter documented a significant fact: General Cos told Dr. Patrick that Crockett was captured and then executed. When considered with statements of the other eyewitnesses, the letter provides additional evidence that Crockett did survive the fighting.[35]

Until 1955, however, available sources really afforded little reason for historians to believe that Crockett was murdered by Santa Anna's order. The early accounts by Urissa and Becerra have a ring of folklore instead of history, and Zuber's letter mentioning General Cos certainly lends no credence to the story. But in 1955 came the publication in Mexico, in original Spanish, of Lieutenant Colonel de la Peña's diary. In the years following, additional documentation appeared. Besides de la Peña's translated narrative, two other valid eyewitness account have been published in

[35] W. P. Zuber to Charlie Jeffries, "Inventing Stories about the Alamo," in *In the Shadow of History* (Austin, 1939), pp. 42–47; W. P. Zuber, "Eighty Years in Texas: Reminiscences of a Texas Veteran from 1830 to 1910" (manuscript), pp. 208–214, Texas State Archives, Austin; W. P. Zuber, "The Escape of Rose from the Alamo," *The Quarterly of the Texas State Historical Association*, 5: 5; 6: 68; R. B. Blake, "A Vindication of Rose and His Story," in *In the Shadow of History*, pp. 29–34.

the United States since 1960. These accounts, in addition to the basic facts of Crockett's death as told in *Exploits and Adventures* and now known to be based 'on a participant's recollections, create a massive body of evidence.

An eyewitness account of another San Jacinto prisoner of war (a high-ranking but unknown officer), appeared in the August, 1960, issue of the *Journal of Southern History*. The account was originally published in the *Detroit Democratic Free Press* of September 7, 1836.

George M. Dolson, a sergeant in the Texas army, included the account in a letter written to his brother in Detroit on July 19, 1836, only a few months after Santa Anna's defeat at San Jacinto. On the day before, Dolson had interpreted a statement made by a Mexican officer, unfortunately unidentified, describing Crockett's death.

The officer was quoted as saying, ". . . on the morning the Alamo was captured, between the hours of five and six o'clock, General Castrillon, who fell at the battle of San Jacinto, entered the back room of the Alamo, and there found Crockett and five other Americans, who had defended it until defence was useless." Castrillón restrained his soldiers and marched the captives before Santa Anna after promising to save them.

Dolson continued the officer's account: "Colonel

Crockett was in the rear, had his arms folded, and appeared bold as the lion as he passed my informant. Almonte, Santa Anna's interpreter, knew Colonel Crockett, and said to my informant, 'the one behind is the famous Crockett.'" Santa Anna reprimanded Castrillón and commanded his soldiers to shoot the prisoners.

The officer's straightforward statement provides details found in no other source. Significantly, he was not quoted as saying that Crockett or the others had surrendered.[36]

The second source to appear in print in the 1960's was not so lengthy or so clear as Dolson's letter. It is part of the evidence, however, and should be included

[36] Conelly, "Did David Crockett Surrender at the Alamo?" pp. 368–376. Dolson's informant has been erroneously identified as Juan Nepomuceno Almonte because one sentence of the letter has been garbled in transcription. As given, it reads,". . . appeared bold as the lion as he passed my informant (Almonte). Santa Anna's interpreter knew Colonel Crockett. . . ." This rendering does not make sense, and the passage should read, ". . . appeared bold as the lion as he passed my informant. Almonte, Santa Anna's interpreter, knew Colonel Crockett. . . ." Almonte was educated in the United States and certainly would not have had a man only a few months in Texas translate for him. He was, in fact, Santa Anna's interpreter and not only interpreted for him with General Houston after San Jacinto but also later accompanied his chief to Washington as aide and interpreter. See "Juan Nepomuceno Almonte," in *The Handbook of Texas*, ed. Walter Prescott Webb, 2 vols. (Austin, 1952), I, 35; and Ann Fears Crawford (ed.), *The Eagle: The Autobiography of Santa Anna* (Austin, 1967), pp. 55–57.

with the other eyewitness accounts. A brief statement about Crockett's death is included in the translated excerpts from the memoirs of Lieutenant Colonel José Juan Sánchez Navarro which were published in Mexico in 1966 and in the United States in 1968.

Sánchez Navarro, who led the assault on the Alamo at the head of the first column under General Cos, wrote, "By six-thirty in the morning not a single enemy existed. . . . Some cruelties horrified me, among them the death of an oldster (*anciano*) whom they called Cocran. . . ."

Sánchez Navarro did not know English, and he could easily have mistaken "Crockett" for "Cocran." A Robert Cochran was indeed an Alamo defender, but Crockett, at age fifty, would better fit the description of *anciano* than the twenty-six-year-old Cochran. In 1836 many men were old at fifty years. Furthermore, Colonel Urissa also referred to Crockett as an old man. Fatigue from the stress of battle could have given him the appearance of age far beyond his fifty years.[37]

Although the eyewitnesses agree that Santa Anna

[37] Miguel A. Sanchez Lamego, *The Siege and Taking of the Alamo*, trans. Consuelo Velasco (Santa Fe, 1968), p. 37; Carlos Sanchez Navarro, *La Guerra de Tejas: Memorias de un soldado* (Mexico, 1960), p. 84; Amelia Williams, "A Critical Study of the Siege of the Alamo and of the Personnel of Its Defenders," *Southwestern Historical Quarterly* 37: 252.

uttered the fatal order for the execution of the Texans, none of the general's personal writings even hint at the incident. But Santa Anna would have sought, of course, to avoid mentioning that it ever occurred. In his official report dictated at eight o'clock that morning, the general said he had viewed the corpses of Travis, Bowie, and Crockett, but he added nothing more. Santa Anna devoted only one paragraph of his autobiography to the assault on the Alamo and pointedly said, ". . . not one soldier showed signs of desiring to surrender, and with fierceness and valor, they died fighting." All indications are that he tried to absolve himself of any blame for the heartless executions.[38]

Not one report of an eyewitness has been found by Alamo scholars to support the popular notion that Crockett went down while desperately clubbing Mexican soldiers with the barrel of his shattered rifle. Nonetheless, most historians have concluded from statements made by two known "Texian" survivors of the battle (neither of whom witnessed the event) that he died fighting.

Mrs. Almeron Dickenson, widowed during the attack, lay in hiding clutching her infant daughter while the fighting raged. She gave her version of the

[38] Day, *Texas Almanac*, pp. 611–613; Crawford, *The Eagle*, p. 51.

battle numerous times throughout the years. The other survivor, who has lived through history simply as "Joe," was the twenty-one-year-old slave of Colonel Travis. Joe also remained hidden during the fighting. Later he accompanied the grieving Mrs. Dickenson and her baby to bear the tragic news to the Texas army as it fell back before the advancing Mexicans.

Both Mrs. Dickenson and Joe assumed that Crockett died in hand-to-hand combat. They related almost identical stories. Both told of being discovered in their hiding places by an English-speaking officer. Each suffered slight wounds during capture. Both witnessed the killing of a Texas gunner named Walker. Mexican soldiers must have found both at about the same time and place, near the end of the bloodiest fighting.

Even their earliest recorded statements reflected heavy editorial assistance aimed at building the Crockett legend. The *Telegraph and Texas Register* of March 24, 1836, reported Mrs. Dickenson as saying, "The end of David Crockett of Tennessee, the great hunter of the west, was as glorious as his career . . . had been useful. He and his companions were found surrounded by piles of assailants, whom they had immolated on the altar of Texas liberties." In a later interview she was quoted as saying, "I recognized Col. Crockett lying dead and mutilated between the church and two story barrack building, and even remember seeing his peculiar cap lying by his side."[39] Joe appeared before cabinet members of the infant Republic of Texas on March 20, 1836, and a northern newspaper quoted him: "Crockett, the kind hearted, brave David Crockett, and a few of the devoted friends who entered the Fort with him, were found lying together, with 24 of the slain enemy around him."[40]

Whatever the two survivors observed while being escorted through Santa Anna's milling troops would have been seen under intense stress and even in the shadow of imminent death. Both said simply that they saw the bodies of Crockett and several others lying in the open yard. Both described the scene as it would appear if Crockett and others had been brought before Santa Anna and executed.

The facts related by Mrs. Dickenson and Joe, then, can be considered actually to lend additional support to the version told by the Mexican soldiers. Mrs. Dickenson's statement that she saw Crockett's body "mutilated" adds further substance. Since both passed through the Alamo yard just as the battle ended, and neither saw Crockett alive, their stories indicate that

[39] J. M. Morphis, *History of Texas* (New York, 1875), p. 177.

[40] *Harrisburg* (Pennsylvania) *Reporter and State Journal*, May 20, 1836. The report must have been written by William F. Gray, for it is given verbatim in his *From Virginia to Texas, 1835* (1965 reprint; Houston, 1909), pp. 136–138.

41

the Texas soldiers must have been executed immediately after their capture.

As for the stories of Crockett turning up alive after the Alamo's fall, most may be dismissed immediately. One tale with apparent documentation continues to surface occasionally and is often confused with eyewitness accounts. The documentation consists of several 1840 newspaper articles.

The story originated with a letter written by a "William C. White" and printed in the *Austin City Gazette* of March 18, 1840. White, who said he lived in Mexico, wrote of a visit to Guadalajara, where a Mexican told him about a Texas prisoner forced to work in a mine. According to White, the prisoner was none other than Crockett, who had been taken alive and sent to Mexico. White said he visited Crockett, who wrote a letter to his family in Tennessee and asked White to mail it for him. White wrote that he mailed the letter in Matamoros and later gave a copy to David L. Wood, a filibuster then serving with Mexican federalists of the Republic of the Rio Grande.

The *City Gazette* editor published White's letter, but expressed his suspicions about its reliability. In the April 1, 1840, issue, that same editor exposed a hoax. He had proved the letter from "William C. White" to be in the handwriting of David L. Wood.

The story spread much faster than its refutation.

Niles' National Register reprinted "White's" letter on April 25, 1840, but did not reveal it as a fraud until June 6. Meanwhile, the news naturally aroused the hopes of John Crockett, David's son, who was then a congressman from Tennessee. The Crockett family had never received the letter supposedly mailed from Matamoros, but John Crockett wanted more details. He sent the U.S. secretary of state a request (dated April 30) that the minister to Mexico investigate the report. John Crockett wrote, "While Santa Anna was a prisoner in Texas, I am informed, he stated to a number of gentlemen, that he [Crockett] was saved alive by Alcuante [*sic*], and that he, Santa Anna, ordered him put to death after it was all over."[41] The false letter apparently raised John Crockett's hopes to the extent that he started for Mexico in search of his father.[42]

Wood's motives in fabricating the hoax are not clear. He arrived in Texas in early 1839 armed with a letter to Mirabeau B. Lamar from the Illinois secretary of state, who praised Wood's ability as a young editor and as a naturalist of "the first Respectability." Wood soon began publishing the "first literary paper in Texas," the *Richmond Telescope and Texas Literary Mes-*

[41] Frederick C. Chabot (ed.) *Texas Letters*, Yanaguana Society Publications, Vol. 5 (San Antonio, 1940), pp. 73–74.

[42] Ibid., pp. 73–75; John H. Jenkins (ed.), "Did Davy Crockett Survive the Alamo?" *Texana* 1: 284–288; Shackford, *David Crockett*, p. 239; Conelly, "Did David Crockett Surrender?" p. 371.

senger, in which he aspired to combine "literary and scientific matter" with "general subjects . . . of interest and utility." Apparently he edited the paper for only a few weeks before resigning because his associate in the venture wished to "promulgate political principles repugnant" to Wood's feelings. Some time later a grand jury indicted Wood for the crime of miscegenation. He might have gone to Mexico in the cause of liberty, to live in peace with his true love, or to avoid prosecution. Whatever provoked him to fabricate the strange tale about Crockett in Mexico is open to even greater speculation.[43]

Wood's hoax, nevertheless, was more believable than the flood of Davy Crockett myths and legends that began to circulate after the Alamo's fall. The folk character that Crockett himself had nurtured assumed truly heroic proportions with his death, largely through the torrent of Crockett almanacs that recounted his mythical and often superhuman adventures. Beginning with the first one in 1835, while Crockett was yet alive, the almanacs steadily issued forth until at least fifty had appeared before the publication of the final one in 1856.[44] In more recent years the legendary Davy has

    [43] Charles Adam Gulick, Jr., et al. (eds.), *The Papers of Mirabeau Buonaparte Lamar*, 6 vols. (Austin, 1920–1927), V, 244, 271, 280–281, 291; Harold Schoen, "The Free Negro in the Republic of Texas," *Southwestern Historical Quarterly* 40: 170.
    [44] Constance Rourke, *Davy Crockett* (1962 reprint; New

been reincarnated by John Wayne in the motion picture *The Alamo* and by Fess Parker in the Walt Disney television series.

With all this fervent publicity that has elevated Crockett to the "King of Wild Frontier," it is little wonder that serious historians have not emphasized the circumstances of the hero's death. Authors of most major works on Texas history seem to agree that Santa Anna's soldiers captured and later executed several Texans at the Alamo, but few include Crockett among them. The majority of the authors devote little space to his death—if they mention it at all. The most common reference made is a simple statement that Crockett's body was found surrounded by bodies of the fallen enemy. Mrs. Anna Pennybacker, the ultimate authority for generations of earlier Texans, added a flourish in the first edition of her *A New History of Texas for Schools.* She wrote, "Brave Crockett left a score of bodies about him to show his work."[45] In some later revisions, however, she dropped any mention of his death.

A primary reason for the brevity regarding Crockett's role at the Alamo is that surprisingly few thorough

York, 1934), pp. 234–237. A writer in one of the almanacs described how Crockett feigned death during the battle and then later avenged his executed comrades by killing their slayers with his hunting knife (ibid., p. 217).

[45] Anna J. Hardwicke Pennybacker, *A New History of Texas for Schools* (Tyler, 1888), p. 78.

studies have been made about the Alamo's defense and fall. Almost a century elapsed after the battle before Amelia Williams compiled her massive *A Critical Study of the Siege of the Alamo*. She assumed from Mrs. Dickenson's account that Crockett fell while fighting not far from the church.[46] Lon Tinkle, in *13 Days to Glory*, also followed Mrs. Dickenson, but he expressed doubt that any Texans were captured. He classed the story that Crockett surrendered along with those legends about the escape of Crockett.[47]

At least two other contemporary authors have examined the now-available Mexican sources and say that Crockett might indeed have been taken, then killed. Walter Lord, whose diligent research and careful appraisal of original sources make his *A Time to Stand* the best recent study of the Alamo, mentions that two of the most reliable eyewitnesses said Crockett was one of the murdered captives. In an epilogue entitled "Riddles of the Alamo," Lord discusses the various eyewitness accounts and concludes that it is indeed possible that Crockett surrendered.[48] The second contemporary author, Richard G. Santos, who wrote *Santa Anna's Campaign against Texas, 1835–1836*, based in part on the general's order book of field commands, points out

[46] Amelia Williams, "A Critical Study of the Siege of the Alamo," p. 43.

[47] Tinkle, *13 Days to Glory*, pp. 221, 224.

[48] Lord, *A Time to Stand*, pp. 175, 206.

that four of Santa Anna's men identified Crockett as one of the unfortunates killed after the battle.[49]

Little doubt now remains that Mexican troops captured several Texans in the final moments of the storming of the Alamo. Statements from seven of Santa Anna's men who were present as eyewitnesses say specifically that David Crockett was one of those taken alive. A reconstruction of the final drama thus can be drawn from the accounts of those who observed it.

As the assault waned about six o'clock that morning of March 6, 1836, General Castrillón found Crockett and several others and marched them into the open Alamo yard. (It deserves repeating here that the most creditable of the eyewitnesses did not say the Texans surrendered.) Santa Anna had entered the blood-soaked grounds to address his assembling troops, and his reply to Castrillón's plea for mercy for the surviving Texans was immediate and terribly final. Soldiers still in the grip of battle fever sprang to execute his order of death. The evidence suggests that the entire episode— from the discovery of the Texans until their deaths— took place within only a few minutes.

The author of what has become known as the definitive biography of Crockett, James Shackford, did not have access to the best of these eyewitness accounts.

[49] Santos, *Santa Anna's Campaign against Texas*, pp. 76 n. 73, 84.

Shackford accepted the story of an alleged Alamo survivor, Madam Candelaria, although he admitted that no one will ever know whether she was actually present inside the Alamo. He simply wrote, "David's death was quite undramatic . . . he was one of the first to fall . . . and he died unarmed."[50]

Shackford's interests rightfully lay more in the man than in the legends, and in summing up Crockett's death, he composed this moving epitaph:

Too much has been made over the details of *how* David died at the Alamo. Such details are not important. What is important is that he died as he had lived. His life was one of indomitable bravery; his death was a death of intrepid courage. His life was one of wholehearted dedication to his concepts of liberty. He died staking his life against what he regarded as intolerable tyranny. A poor man who had long known the devastating consequences of poverty and who all his life had fought a dedicated fight for the right of the dispossessed to a new opportunity, he died defending a poor and insecure people and proclaiming their rights to participate in the arts of self-government. . . . This is the true significance of the death and rebirth of David Crockett.[51]

[50] Shackford, *David Crockett*, pp. 229, 234.
[51] Ibid., pp. 238–239.

. . . And Why Do We Care So Much?

JAMES E. CRISP

LIFE OF
COLONEL DAVID CROCKETT.

DEATH OF COLONEL CROCKETT.

Dan Kilgore and His
Big Little Book

"Looking at Dan Kilgore's slender volume," mused Archie Mc-
Donald from his editor's desk in Nacogdoches, " . . . you wonder
How Did Dan Stir Up Such a Mess?"[1] It's hard to take at face
value Kilgore's protestations that he had no intention of stirring
up any such mess, especially when one reads on the front page
of the *London Daily Mail* of April 28, 1978—only a week after
the appearance of *How Did Davy Die?*—that Dan, because of his
"murder of a myth," was suddenly in danger of becoming "the
most hated man in America."[2]

Yet Thomas H. Kreneck, Kilgore's friend and literary biographer, insists that Dan, far from courting controversy, simply sought to perform the basic but crucial historical exercise of
bringing together, for the first time, all of the "reasonably reliable
eyewitnesses on Crockett's death."[3] His goal, Kilgore intimated
to *Texas Monthly* not long after his book was published, was to
"settle an acrimonious feud among historians once and for all."

The magazine's editors thought that the odds were against him.[4]
They were right.

The Origin and Impact of How Did Davy Die?

The roots of Kilgore's predicament may be found in the
1950s, when myth, documentary evidence, and Dan's love affair
with history assumed trajectories that would bring all three into
collision two decades later.

First, the myth. Those of us now reaching our sixties have
no trouble remembering the Davy Crockett craze that swept
across America following the death of Walt Disney's televised
hero (portrayed by Fess Parker) as he defended the Alamo on
a winter's night in February 1955.[5] The orgy of consumerism
that followed—with everything from the iconic coonskin caps
to ladies' underwear selling out if only they were embossed with
Crockett's magic name—did not last the year.[6] But the heroic
image of Davy's last-ditch defense against hordes of Mexican soldiers was more firmly fixed than ever in the public's mind, leav-
ing many ill disposed to the outcome of Dan's careful examination of the sources. His widow, Carol Kilgore, recalled in 1998
the angry responses to her husband's book twenty years earlier:
"They were just outraged and didn't want to believe their hero
hadn't died swinging [his rifle] Old Betsy."[7]

Next, the evidence. Little noticed by any but the most ar-
dent Alamo aficionados at the time was another event in early
1955: the publication in Mexico City of *La Rebelión de Texas,*

a memoir based on the diary of Mexican officer José Enrique de la Peña, who claimed to have seen with his own eyes exactly how Davy died.[8] Though it remains even today the only detailed description of Crockett's death composed by an alleged eyewitness, the "de la Peña diary" had little immediate impact on either Texan historiography or the American image of Crockett.

Lon Tinkle, in the bibliographical section of his popular 1958 account of the siege of the Alamo, *Thirteen Days to Glory*, called the memoir one of "the most interesting contributions to Alamo investigation in recent years." However, it is unlikely that Tinkle was actually familiar with the book, since he failed to mention the title and incorrectly listed both the date of publication and the author's name (he called him "Gonzalez Pena"). Moreover, Tinkle totally ignored de la Peña's version of Crockett's death.[9]

The far more meticulous historian Walter Lord may have raised a few eyebrows when he incorporated de la Peña's description of the Alamo executions into his best-selling 1961 narrative, *A Time to Stand*. But Lord hedged his bet: he didn't show Crockett dying in his text, and only in his "Riddles of the Alamo" section in the back of the book did he raise even the possibility that Davy might have been among these victims of Santa Anna's wrath.[10]

As awareness of and interest in the de la Peña account grew among Texas researchers in the 1960s, Carmen Perry, a native of Mexico who was then the director of the Daughters of the Republic of Texas Library at the Alamo, began work on an English translation of *La Rebelión de Texas*.[11] Publication did not quickly follow, however, because the widow of Mexican editor Jesús Sánchez Garza proved "totally uncooperative" in granting the rights for a translation—fearing, she told Perry, an "international controversy."[12]

Texas collector and philanthropist John Peace came to the rescue in May 1974, when at Carmen Perry's entreaty he bought the extensive de la Peña manuscripts from the widow and carried them out of Mexico in a battered suitcase, declaring them to customs officials as "old papers." Peace gave full permission to Perry to translate and publish the memoir, but he never saw the result; he died three months after returning to Texas.[13]

The finished product appeared in the fall of 1975. *With Santa Anna in Texas: A Personal Narrative of the Revolution* was one of the first two books published by Texas A&M University Press after its founding in 1974 by Frank Wardlaw.[14] The English-language publication of the de la Peña memoir, however, was a mixed blessing for Carmen Perry. True, the Sons of the Republic of Texas awarded her the Summerfield G. Roberts Award for the outstanding book of 1975, and the following year she was inducted into the prestigious Texas Institute of Letters.[15] But in the meantime, a sensational and egregiously misleading headline in *People* magazine screamed to the nation that Carmen Perry was denying that David Crockett had died in the Alamo.[16] When Perry first saw this issue of the magazine, she had just stopped at a service station in San Antonio; she became so outraged that she couldn't sign the ticket for the gas.[17]

It got worse. *Texas Monthly* bestowed a 1975 Bum Steer Award on her translation, and soon she had what she called a "suitcase . . . full of clippings accusing *me* of all sorts of things I'm supposed to have said about David Crockett."[18] Then there were the poison pen letters in her mailbox and "disruptive and disturbing telephone calls at all hours," including a wake-up call from a Milwaukee radio station looking for a hot story. When Perry protested that she couldn't even talk at seven o'clock in the morning, the voice on the other end of the line informed her that she was already on the air![19]

Dan Kilgore didn't know it, but he had all this and more to look forward to in his own hitherto quiet life as an accountant and amateur historian. Yet from his perspective in 1975, the commotion over the de la Peña narrative actually appeared as the answer to a prayer. He had recently been elected as vice-president (and presumptive president-elect) of the Texas State Historical Association (TSHA), which meant that he needed a suitable topic for the customary valedictory presidential address that he would have to give at the annual meeting of the TSHA in March 1977.[20] Why not take advantage of the fortuitous timing of Perry's work by conducting the "simple historical exercise" of compiling and comparing this and all other existing eyewitness accounts of Crockett's death?[21]

Kilgore was an unlikely candidate for the role of cutting-edge historian. Born on a family farm near Dallas in 1921, Dan was a no-nonsense child of the Great Depression who actually avoided taking history courses at the University of Texas, where he graduated with a business administration degree in 1943.[22] Settling into an accounting firm in Corpus Christi after the war, Dan was unwittingly bitten by the history bug in 1947 when he and a friend gambled on buying a couple of boxes of unclaimed freight, which turned out to be books. Dan's hidden treasures were only children's literature, but as a newcomer to South Texas he was curious about the local histories found in his friend's carton. Dan ultimately purchased them, and within three or four years Kilgore had "a bad case of book fever" as he filled shelves with the fruits of his new avocation.[23]

Dan was no mere collector. By the end of the 1950s he was writing historical pieces for the Corpus Christi newspaper that were calling into question certain beloved local traditions. Kilgore had the audacity to insist on documentation.[24] By the time he came to the attention of the *Houston Chronicle* in 1961, Kilgore was president of the South Texas Historical Association and making a name for himself by a "demand for accuracy" that set him apart from most amateurs. "The truth is," he told the *Chronicle,* "that a tremendous amount of South Texas legendry has come to be accepted as history. It tends, sometimes, to make things confusing for the historian."[25] Dan was falling in love not just with history books, but also with the primary sources from which reliable history is crafted.

By 1973 Dan had already published his first volume, *A Ranger Legacy: 150 Years of Service to Texas,* as his interest in local legend Sally Scull (a female cotton freighter and horse trader) led him to the discovery of her relatives' exploits in the very earliest years of the rangers in Stephen F. Austin's colony.[26] Dan was also digging deeply into some of the classic historical mysteries of early Texas as he corresponded in the 1960s with scholars in Mexico and the Library of Congress about obscure sources describing the executions at the Alamo and the death of David Crockett.[27]

In message and structure, the speech that Kilgore prepared for the TSHA meeting of March 4, 1977, was not essentially different from what became the little book *How Did Davy Die?*[28] Those who heard the talk reported a compelling and well-crafted presidential address that "caused little, if any, consternation."[29] Carmen Perry had unfortunately missed the meeting but quickly got wind of Kilgore's "very interesting . . . farewell speech" and wrote him on March 14 requesting a copy. She also included an implicit warning, telling Kilgore about that suitcase full of accusatory clippings that she had received after publishing the de la Peña memoir.[30]

Her warning came a bit too late. Frank Wardlaw, director of Texas A&M University Press, was in the banquet room at the Baker Hotel in Dallas when Kilgore gave the speech, and after dinner he strode directly to the head table to ask Dan if he would like to publish an expanded version of his essay as a book.[31] Kilgore readily agreed, but after spending the next few months polishing his prose and sharpening his citations, he was ready for a break. Dan sent the signed contract and the completed manuscript to Wardlaw on October 30 with this unintended bit of irony: "To be honest, I am a little weary of Davy and hope we can soon put him to rest."[32]

Kilgore maintained for the rest of his life that "It never occurred to [him] that there would be controversy."[33] He certainly didn't have long to wait to be proven wrong. The first press release from the publisher describing *How Did Davy Die?* was drafted on April 20, 1978, and distributed the next day— San Jacinto Day.[34] And just like Santa Anna exactly 142 years earlier, beginning that very day Dan was surprised, placed on the defensive, and a bit overwhelmed by an assault that really should have been expected.

Kilgore had traveled to Austin on that anniversary of the Battle of San Jacinto to appear on Cactus Pryor's radio show; Dan later recalled that the telephone messages started piling up even before he and his wife, Carol, had made it back to Corpus Christi.[35] A reporter for the *San Antonio Light* caught up with them when they stopped in the Alamo city to spend the night with an aunt on their way home, and Dan's defensiveness is obvious in the final quote from the story that appeared the next day: "I want to stress that I am not trying to run down Crockett," he protested. "I am just trying to present the documentary evidence on an incident in Texas history."[36]

The tone and direction of the interview in San Antonio may be inferred from Kilgore's serially quoted replies to the reporter's questions: "It appears he was either captured or he surrendered." "However, there is no real proof that he surrendered." "But even if he did surrender, I could hardly see anything shameful in it."[37] Dan went on to point out the importance of the mutually corroborative statements of the seven Mexican soldiers that constituted the heart of his book, but he must have realized early on that he was going to be haunted by that San Jacinto Day press release.

As he tried to come to terms with the surge of negative publicity that engulfed him over the next few weeks and months, Kilgore often put the blame on the "Associated Press rewrite man in Dallas who transformed the release prior to placing it on the national wire."[38] This guy, claimed Kilgore, had really "worked it over," but the transformation consisted mainly of replacing the first sentence of the story with a line that would grab the attention of newspaper editors across the country. Instead of the original opening—"Facts seem to be catching up with the legend of Davy Crockett"—the piece now commenced with this little gem: "Any Texan worth his pointy-toed, ringtail lizard–skin cowboy boots knows better than to smear the legend of Davy Crockett."[39]

Yet the debunking negativity of the original A&M press release—which drew its content mainly from the opening pages of *How Did Davy Die?*—may be grasped by a list of its strikingly downbeat words and phrases: "less heroic than popularly believed," "dismal career," "failed financially," "less than liberty-loving," "tragic finale," "failure in achievement of worldly goals," "poor man," "undistinguished record," "shame suffered when he was defeated [for] Congress," and "not with any idea of dying for the liberty of Texas." Only the last two of a total of sixteen paragraphs in the press release dealt with Kilgore's examination of the documentary evidence. Far more prominent was its first quotation, from Dan's own text: "Crockett's heroism seemed to expand in direct proportion to the distance news had to travel about him."[40]

This all was too much for one very tightly wound Alabaman, who took pen to paper the day the story hit the wire. He sent a long, intense letter addressed to "Dan Kilgore—accountant," suggesting that the "Corpus Christi mathematician" who had authored this "behemoth narrative" calling Crockett's heroism into question was a nothing more than a "mealy-mouthed intellectual C.P.A. [who] should at the first opportunity have his mouth washed out with soap."[41] A few days later, when Dan ventured onto a Memphis, Tennessee, radio call-in show, he was subjected to more angry, rambling accusations, including the charge that he was nothing but a "smut peddler."[42]

By May 3, less than two weeks after the book was published, Frank Wardlaw (with tongue firmly in cheek) gave these instructions to those preparing a book signing party for Kilgore in Corpus Christi: "If you think Dan needs police protection, please arrange it."[43] Kilgore was at the center of a media frenzy that he found amusing, perplexing, and disturbing all at the same time. What got his goat more than anything else was that his critics not only weren't buying How Did Davy Die?—they probably had never seen it.

There was one critic in particular who angered Dan: Austin author John R. Knaggs, who (Kilgore believed) had not only jumped into the fray without reading the book but also had done so in order to sell his own recently published novel of the Texas

Revolution, *The Bugles Are Silent.*[44] A long, unsigned article extensively quoting Knaggs appeared in the April 28, 1977, issue of *The Austin Citizen,* a paper for which Knaggs sat on the board of directors.[45] A UPI story in the *Dallas Morning News* with an Austin dateline, summarizing the Knaggs critique of Kilgore's work, appeared on the very same day, as did a news release from the publisher of the Knaggs novel, touting its accuracy and dismissing Kilgore's argument out of hand (but without reference to Dan's actual evidence).[46]

Dan was steamed. When a reporter for the *Wall Street Journal* asked him about the Knaggs "rebuttal," the journalist (as Kilgore confided later to Wardlaw) "hit a sensitive spot and I said some bad words."[47] Dan followed up with a long letter to the reporter, noting that Knaggs (a former state capitol UPI correspondent) had either planted or written the story and then "had a buddy send it out over the UPI wire," where it received wide circulation. Dan complained that Knaggs was "promoting his novel at my expense" and criticizing a book he had never read.[48] Kilgore believed in, and practiced, a stern work ethic. In handwritten notes to himself about his sources and his critics, Dan wrote that "Knaggs . . . did his research with his mouth, a technique I never learned."[49]

Kilgore was equally angered by another writer whose methodologies were very much unlike his own. Roger Simon was a columnist for the *Chicago Sun-Times* who seems to have used his fifteen-minute telephone interview with Dan as inspiration rather than documentation. As a still irked Kilgore told an interviewer in 1986, "[Simon] used my book as an opportunity to make up all sorts of things, such as how Crockett's personal motto was 'Victory, or how about another chance on Tuesday?' or 'Be sure you're right, then lie about it.'"[50]

Some Texas newspapers heavily censored Simon's column, but even the *Houston Chronicle,* which excised virtually all of the wise-guy improvisations, left in a couple of loaded sentences that many of its readers erroneously attributed to Kilgore: "The reason that Crockett and the other 181 brave souls were at the Alamo in the first place is very simple. They were there to steal the land from the Mexicans who legally owned the place." Moreover, Simon put some fightin' words directly into Dan's mouth that he never actually uttered. According to the column, "Kilgore says that Davy Crockett was a flop and a fink and maybe a coward to boot."[51]

Once again, Kilgore had been warned in advance by Carmen Perry. She had written him a week before the Simon column appeared, commiserating with him now that he shared her "guilt" and noting that all of the caustic comments about *How Did Davy Die?* in clippings that she had recently received made it "quite obvious that [the critics] had not read the book." She expressed the sentiment, no doubt soon shared by Kilgore, "that something could be done with the *Press* to keep it from misinforming the public on so many issues. I don't believe anything I read in the papers anymore."[52]

Dan had readily shared with Roger Simon the first angry

letter that he had received, the one from Alabama addressed to the "mealy-mouthed intellectual" who should have his mouth washed out with soap. Kilgore noted that it also contained an implicit threat more dire than soap. Alluding to "white-Southern men, age 17 on" (and perhaps attempting to describe himself as well as Crockett), the writer had proclaimed: "Countenance is excellent, keen eyesight, healthy, and indeed will battle it out with you, fists, knives, guns or will climb up on the roof of a Texas-based Church [and] fight in front of God, women & everybody."[53] Perhaps remembering Carmen Perry's warning, Kilgore told Simon, "Now that's some letter," then he added: "But I am expecting worse."[54]

He got it. As he told Frank Wardlaw on June 24, just as "the tumult and shouting seem[ed] to die, [it] resurrect[ed]."[55] Dan had appeared to be rather amused as he told Roger Simon about the Alabama letter, and he confided to an interviewer many years later his feeling that the letter writer was "nutty."[56] But the Simon column stimulated responses that became progressively less easy to dismiss. Yet, as Perry put it, it was still "quite obvious that they had not read the book."

One unwelcome correspondent, Frank M. Dyer of Houston, came right out with it: "At this juncture I personally have not read your book." Rather than springing for the five-dollar purchase price, Dyer instead hammered out a letter of more than three single-spaced pages, demanding satisfaction on "several points that vex me." He made no distinction between Simon's silliness and Kilgore's actual claims.[57]

The questions Dyer was demanding answers to were a bit opaque, but the insults hurled at Kilgore were not. "Being a controversial and notorious fool is not what I would think you would desire for yourself" was a typical taunt. He suggested that Kilgore take a "junior college survey course in almost any period of any history" and added that he "assume[d] that one need not be a serious student of the history of Texas in order to belong to or be an officer in the Texas State Historical Society." His follow-up question to Kilgore was: "Am I correct in that assumption?"[58]

The next missive from Houston could not be as easily filed away and forgotten as Dyer's harangue. It took the form of an angry letter to the editor of the *Houston Chronicle* on May 17, ten days after that newspaper had printed the heavily edited version of Simon's column. The writer found the "statements about Davy Crockett" to be "part of a pattern to discredit and disgrace all prominent white Americans who helped to build our state and nation." He charged that "lies have been concocted and facts distorted to make all white American heroes appear to be fugitives from morals charges or rank cowards at the least." After challenging Kilgore and Simon to help defend America from an "invasion" of "Mexicans, Hindus, Chinese," and half a dozen other threatening foreign groups, the bitter Houstonian defended the "ownership" rights of "white Texans vs. Mexicans" and "white European Afrikaaners vs. migratory black Africans."[59] A week later, Kilgore received a letter from Florida accusing him of being part of a Communist plan to degrade "our [American] hero's [*sic*]."[60]

Dan could joke about being called a communist—not a problem for a politically conservative CPA—but the racial overtones that ran through some of the castigations of his work made him profoundly uncomfortable, and he never referred to this issue publicly.[61] In fact, it would be years before Kilgore could entertain even the idea that the Davy Crockett of myth could be a topic of more significance for American historians than the David Crockett of documented "reality."

In 1978 Dan had expected an extensive scholarly appraisal of his carefully crafted work, but precious little was forthcoming. "All the publicity seems to have killed my reviews," he remarked to Frank Wardlaw toward the end of June.[62] The only exception came from faraway North Texas, where Llerena Friend, who had written the introduction to Carmen Perry's *With Santa Anna in Texas,* published a respectful assessment in her hometown *Wichita Falls Times.*[63] Dan's book ultimately received far fewer reviews in historical journals than had Perry's translation, with only the state quarterlies in Texas, Oklahoma, and Tennessee taking note with generally positive, if perfunctory, reviews.[64]

Years later, recalling the swirling controversy and the philistine harangues that had greeted *How Did Davy Die?* Kilgore would complain with acerbic irony that despite all the anger, "nobody even read the damn book."[65] But readers there were, and Dan's little book grew steadily in influence, even while it remained a lightning rod for Davy's defenders. Eventually, Kilgore would live to see his own maddening experience with irrational criticism incorporated into the story of the Alamo as "a cultural and political symbol," even as his conclusions about Crockett's death were coming to define the story of the Alamo of "historical fact."[66]

Dan and His Sources

In the meantime, the most interesting (though perhaps also the most obscure) review of *How Did Davy Die?* appeared in the December 1982 issue of the newsletter of the Alamo Lore and Myth Organization. Although ALAMO was headquartered in San Antonio, the reviewer, Bill Groneman, was a New York City fire marshal and arson detective and, like Dan Kilgore, an amateur historian.[67] Groneman's interest in Crockett and the Alamo was strong and long-standing. Despite the distance from his home base, the New Yorker had attended Carmen Perry's book signing party celebrating the publication of *With Santa Anna in Texas* at Rosengren's Book Store in San Antonio in October 1975.[68] Moreover, Bill Groneman would eventually become a major participant in what the *Wilson Quarterly* called in 1998 "one of the bloodier skirmishes of the academic culture wars"— the ongoing controversy over Davy's death.[69]

Groneman's 1982 review was actually in the form of a rebuttal—an "answer," as he put it—to the argument and conclusions of *How Did Davy Die?* Expressing a criticism broached by the Alabaman author of Dan's first "hate mail," but in a far more respectful tone, Groneman began his rebuttal by saying that "Mr. Kilgore is an accomplished Historian, but his vocation is that of a Certified Public Accountant, and I feel that he approaches the question of Crockett's death as an accountant."

Groneman explained that what he meant by this was that Dan "merely compiles statements and records, sums them up, and comes to a cut-and-dry conclusion."[70]

This criticism may not have been entirely fair, but Groneman was pointing toward a genuine weakness in Kilgore's presentation of his argument. The careful reader of *How Did Davy Die?* may already have noticed that Dan claims just a bit too much for the testimony of his seven Mexican soldiers when he says (p. 22; the emphasis here is mine) that each of them "*specifically* identified Crockett as one of the captives." He repeats this claim at the end of the book when he says (p. 47; also with my emphasis) that "statements from seven of Santa Anna's men who were present as eyewitnesses say *specifically* that David Crockett was one of those taken alive."

Not exactly. Kilgore's conclusion here is not a statement of literal fact, but rather of Dan's interpretation and opinion. Some of these men certainly referred specifically to David Crockett, but Urissa (p. 23) pointed to "a venerable looking old man" called "Coket" who stooped as he walked, and Sánchez Navarro (p. 38) spoke of a very old man ("*un anciano*") "whom they called Cocran." Dan reasoned that these were likely references by non-English speakers to the name "Crockett." But reviewer Gene Brack may not have been justified when he contended in the *Southwestern Historical Quarterly* that Kilgore's "argument never exceeds its proof."[71]

There was a tendency by Dan and his supporters (though Kilgore did indeed point out that some of his eyewitnesses were more believable than others) to add up the stories of the seven soldiers as if they were *completely* corroborative. This tendency may be seen most clearly in Corpus Christi columnist Bill Walraven's palpably false claim in the midst of the controversy over Dan's book that "the accounts of seven Mexican soldiers . . . all tell the *identical* story."[72] Kilgore himself fell into the same trap when he argued to *Texas Monthly* in the summer of 1978 that "except for a few minor details, the stories are all the same."[73] Looking back on the controversy fifteen years later, his position remained that there were "seven soldiers who said essentially the same thing."[74]

This claim can be true only if one is looking for one thing and one thing only in these testimonies: a statement (as Kilgore puts it on page 35 with regard to General Cos) that "Crockett was captured and then executed." But the seven stories themselves nevertheless varied wildly. Remember that Sergeant Dolson's informant, who very clearly identified Davy among the executed defenders (pp. 36–37), said that "Crockett . . . had his arms folded, and appeared bold as the lion as he passed my informant." This was hardly the stooped old man described by Urissa. Sergeant Becerra, moreover, claimed (pp. 25–26) to have found Travis and Crockett together on the floor of a room where they were identified and offered salvation by General Cos, and Cos allegedly claimed (pp. 32–35) that he (and *not* Castrillón, as Urissa and others reported) was indeed the Mexican general who had tried to save Crockett's life.

The danger here is that to claim specificity for each of the seven soldiers who identified Crockett among the executed, or to advance the even more problematic proposition that all seven of

68

their stories were essentially equivalent, is to come very close to just adding up the alleged eyewitnesses—believable or not—on one side of the ledger and reaching a conclusion that smacks of mathematical certainty. Kilgore was not displaying his characteristic caution when he told *Texas Monthly* in 1978 that there was "absolutely no doubt in [his] mind" that Crockett did not die fighting.[75]

Moreover, the emphasis on seven soldiers all allegedly saying the same thing (when in fact they were not) led Kilgore away from what could have been a more profitable and persuasive comparison of some of these texts with what one might call the gold standard of eyewitnesses to the Alamo executions. This was the account of Ramón Martínez Caro, Santa Anna's personal secretary, whom Dan quotes in *How Did Davy Die?* on pages 16 and 17. As a source almost universally accepted on the Alamo killings, Martínez Caro's account—though it never mentions Crockett—could conceivably hold the key to determining the authenticity of other accounts, provided that one could establish that the origins of those accounts were independent of Martínez Caro's.[76]

In his counterargument to Kilgore, Groneman did employ the comparative approach, choosing to emphasize a striking common element in the eyewitness accounts of three Alamo survivors, two of whom Kilgore (for perhaps good reasons) ignored. Of course, Dan did examine the testimony of Mrs. Almeron Dickenson (pp. 39–41); he ultimately concluded that her testimony actually bolstered the likelihood of Crockett's execution.

The two others examined by Groneman were the alleged Mexican eyewitnesses Captain Rafael Soldana and Sergeant Félix Núñez. Both of these men claimed to have seen an impressive Texan (or "American") marksman during the Alamo fighting. Soldana claims that the man was known as "Kwockey," and Núñez describes in detail this defender's death in close combat with Mexican soldiers.[77]

The common element that led Bill Groneman to weigh these three testimonies more heavily on the scale of likelihood than Dan Kilgore's seven soldiers' accounts was their description of Crockett's clothing, and especially the "peculiar cap" mentioned by Mrs. Dickenson in one of her later interviews. Soldana described "a tall man with flowing hair" wearing "a buckskin suit and a cap all of a pattern entirely different from those worn by his comrades."[78] Núñez reported "a tall American of rather dark complexion" with a "long buckskin coat and a round cap without any bill, made out of fox skin with the long tail hanging down his back."[79] These three accounts, claims Groneman, are "direct, and to the point," adding no "embellishments." When taken together, he argues, "they make a good case for Crockett to have lived up to his legendary status."[80]

In his critical essay, all of Groneman's citations for these three accounts were to the versions of their testimony published in Walter Lord's *A Time to Stand;* thus, Groneman did not attempt to document his counterargument with references to the original sources. This may seem a minor quibble until one begins to see that there is yet another aspect of the stories of the alleged Alamo eyewitnesses—both Groneman's and Kilgore's—that needs to be taken into account: their relative immediacy.

By "immediacy," I mean both the amount of time that has elapsed between the witnessing of the deed and the penning of the tale and the number of intermediaries through whom the story has passed. When subjected to these twin tests of immediacy, the reliability of many of these "eyewitnesses" begins to wither.

Kilgore has described (pp. 32–35) the tortured path to first publication in 1939 taken by the story attributed to General Cos—a story actually repudiated by the man who first put it in writing in 1904. Kilgore has also shown (p. 24) that the "bizarre" story told by Sergeant Francisco Becerra was not written down by Rip Ford until 1875, thirty-nine years after the events at the Alamo transpired. Moreover, Ford admitted in 1895 that the long-dead Becerra was by no means certain of the identities of the men whom he had thought to be Travis and Crockett.[81] But even with this weak competition, Groneman's additional witnesses—Soldana and Núñez—do not look good by comparison when subjected to the test of immediacy.

Historian Stephen L. Hardin notes that the Núñez account has been used by countless historians as an "eyewitness" account of the Alamo despite its glaring errors and doubtful provenance. Until Hardin himself published an annotated version of it in 1990, it had not been published in full since its appearance in the *San Antonio Daily Express* (and its reprinting in the *Fort Worth Gazette*) 101 years earlier. The Núñez story

71

was apparently rewritten by an unnamed newspaper reporter and had previously passed through the hands of a mysterious and unidentified Professor George W. Noel.[82] It is third-hand information at best, and it certainly fails the "immediacy test" in terms of the passage of time between the events and their recording. It would, concludes Hardin, be "folly to use any part of it to support an argument."[83]

The Soldana story also bears a dubious provenance. It was "set down and written out" by James T. DeShields, who claimed to have heard the story directly from the Texan Revolutionary soldier Creed Taylor, who in turn claimed to have met Soldana and heard his tale "at Corpus Christi shortly after the close of the Mexican War."[84] What DeShields did not tell his readers is that he had purchased the Taylor reminiscences for two hundred dollars from John W. Hunter, a teacher and newspaperman who did in fact interview Creed Taylor but who had fallen onto hard times and could not publish the manuscript himself. DeShields heavily reworked the Taylor/Hunter material and did not acknowledge Hunter's role in producing the work. Thus, the Soldana account is at best fourth-hand, and in any case was not written down in any form until Hunter's 1891 interviews with Taylor.[85]

The problem with the use of such problematic sources—by either Kilgore or Groneman—is obvious: each is looking for stories, or even fragments of near-preposterous stories, that will bolster one side or the other of the narrow argument over whether Crockett was executed. What can get lost in this process is an appreciation for the degree to which sources can be corroborative in a more holistic way than is shown by their agreement on a single point. A more comprehensive examination of sources that questions their "immediacy" (in both senses of that term) and that compares them more fully to other accounts of accepted reliability will in the end create a more effective argument than one resting on a misplaced emphasis on the total number of alleged eyewitnesses.

It is useful at this point to return to an often overlooked statement that Dan Kilgore made on page 35 of *How Did Davy Die?*: "Until 1955 . . . available sources [such as those attributed to Urissa, Cos, and Becerra] really afforded little reason to believe that Crockett was murdered by Santa Anna's order." In other words, most of the early evidence was defective and hardly persuasive. In addition to the de la Peña memoir that appeared in 1955, says Kilgore (p. 36), two other sources appeared in the United States in the 1960s that, "when added to the basic facts of Crockett's death as told in the *Exploits and Adventures* and now known to be based on a participant's recollections [see pp. 19–21], create a massive body of evidence."

These two other new sources were the "Dolson Letter" and the account of Lieutenant Colonel José Juan Sánchez Navarro; Kilgore devotes two pages (36–37) to the former and only a page (38) to the latter. The brief Sánchez Navarro comment on the cruel death of the "oldster (*anciano*) whom they called Cocran" probably deserves no more attention than this, though in its reliability the Sánchez Navarro account should rank far

73

above such compromised sources as Urissa, Becerra, Núñez, or Soldana. Although Bill Groneman has argued that the Sánchez Navarro journal is likely a forgery, James E. Ivey and Jack Jackson published a definitive refutation of that accusation in 2001. They pointed out that in certain important qualities the Sánchez Navarro document—written directly as a record of daily events by its author—is superior even to the far more famous de la Peña "diary."[86]

This latter document is actually an enlarged memoir based on a recopied diary (from an original diary now lost) that itself does not mention either Crockett or the Alamo executions. The de la Peña account as published by Jesús Sánchez Garza in Mexico and Carmen Perry in Texas was not only rewritten for publication by de la Peña, but by his own admission it also contains descriptions provided by other observers of events not seen by de la Peña himself (although he claims in the memoir to have witnessed the execution of Crockett).[87] Yet in the aftermath of Perry's translation and Kilgore's endorsement of de la Peña's version of Crockett's death, and continuing through and beyond a day-long conference held in April 2000 to celebrate the acquisition of de la Peña's manuscripts by the University of Texas at Austin, it is this Alamo account that has garnered more attention than all of the others combined.[88]

However, it is in the far-less-celebrated letter written by George M. Dolson that we may actually find the best evidence for how Davy Crockett died. Moreover, a reevaluation of this document will allow us to see the historian Dan Kilgore at his meticulous and insightful best. In the lengthy footnote on page 37 of *How Did Davy Die?* Kilgore explains how Dolson's informant had "been erroneously identified as Juan Nepomuceno Almonte because one sentence of the letter has been garbled in transcription." More precisely stated, the newspaper typesetter who transcribed Dolson's handwritten letter very probably put the word "Almonte" (in parentheses) on the wrong side of the period that divides two sentences, changing Almonte's apparent identity from Santa Anna's interpreter to Dolson's unnamed informant, for whom Dolson was serving as translator.

Kilgore was too polite to mention that both Thomas Lawrence Connelly (the graduate student who brought the Dolson Letter to scholars' attention in 1960) and the highly respected Walter Lord (who accepted Connelly's erroneous identification of Dolson's informant as Almonte) simply did not know enough about Almonte's basic biography to realize that the multilingual Mexican colonel would have needed no translator and thus could not have been Dolson's informant.[89] (Moreover, a closer look at Almonte's whereabouts during the Texas Revolution would also have shown that he was never held at the prisoner-of-war camp on Galveston Island, where the interview with the informant took place.)[90]

Why is the Dolson Letter so important? Its timeliness and immediacy are obvious. The interview with the informant took place in the summer of 1836, and Sergeant Dolson wrote down the narrative on the very next day in his letter to his brother in Michigan. But it is the comparison with the account written a year later by Ramón Martínez Caro, Santa Anna's personal secretary, that most effectively bolsters the authenticity of this prisoner's account.

The number of common elements in the two stories, some of which were not mentioned by Kilgore, appear to be beyond mere coincidence: each says that General Manuel Castrillón discovered the defenders in hiding immediately after the battle; each says that Castrillón took the men directly to Santa Anna, who rebuked his subordinate for not having killed the men; each says that the prisoners were immediately dispatched by other soldiers in the presence of Santa Anna.

While Martínez Caro mentioned five captives and Dolson's informant counted six, such a minor discrepancy in their respective accounts after the passage of weeks and months from the incident actually lends more credibility than would a lockstep agreement between the two sources. Moreover, although the Dolson Letter, like the de la Peña account, says that Santa Anna ordered the captured defenders to be shot, none of these three accounts reports that they were actually killed by gunfire. All three are reconcilable with the prisoners' being killed by swords or bayonets.[91]

All of these documents, of course, have their debunkers. Bill Groneman has written that there is "enough nonsense" in the Dolson Letter "to eliminate it as a credible source," but the only nonsense that he mentions is the informant's statement that Crockett and the other prisoners were "marched to the tent of Santa Anna" by General Castrillón.[92] Santa Anna was not using a tent during the siege of the Alamo, nor did he erect one within the walls of the Alamo after the battle. The reference to the tent would indeed be damaging to the account's credibility if the Mexican prisoner-of-war had actually used the words "marched to the tent of Santa Anna," but we know that he did not. The words are in English, and the prisoner spoke only Spanish. That is why Sergeant Dolson was in the room. He was the interpreter.

I am not trying to be overly analytical here, but rather to get to the reality behind this document. What could the prisoner have said that would have led Dolson to think that Santa Anna had a tent in the Alamo plaza? The Spanish word *pabellón* can indeed mean a large tent, but it is also the term used for the national flag of Mexico—not a mere *bandera,* but the official flag of the nation bearing the seal of the government, to be flown only by government entities. If the informant stated that the men were marched "*al pabellón de Santa Anna*" (meaning, "to the flag of Santa Anna"), Dolson (who had arrived in Texas after the Battle of San Jacinto) might well have thought that there had been a tent on the scene, but this is hardly disqualifying "nonsense." In fact, a probable translation error of this kind lends credence to Dolson's story of his service as a Spanish interpreter.[93]

Historian William C. Davis has taken another tack, arguing that Ramón Martínez Caro could have found and plagiarized a newspaper's copy of the Dolson Letter, thus putting a possibly false story in his 1837 memoir.[94] (The letter was indeed reprinted by some newspapers in the United States, though its first notice by historians came only with Thomas Lawrence Connelly's discovery in 1960).[95] What Davis cannot explain, however, is why Martínez Caro would have placed a bogus narrative of the execution of Alamo defenders in a book intended for a Mexican audience—an audience that included officers who had also been present at the battle and who could have called him to task for a false account.

The fact that Martínez Caro did not mention Crockett *could* mean, as Davis has also argued, that Santa Anna's secretary knew Crockett's identity but left out this information because it would have been wasted on a Mexican audience. Yet it is far more likely that unlike Dolson's informant, who says he was clued in by Colonel Almonte to Crockett's presence in the group of captives, Martínez Caro simply did not know the identity of any of the victims whom he saw executed.[96]

Obviously, arguments over specific sources concerning Crockett's fate—even those of such high quality as the Dolson Letter—may be endless. But before taking leave of this key document, we should acknowledge the intellectual independence and agility shown by Dan Kilgore as he identified and corrected the erroneous attribution of the unnamed prisoner's account to Juan Almonte. Keep in mind that this misattribution was made not only by the document's discoverer (Connelly) and the most celebrated historian of the Battle of the Alamo (Lord); precisely the same error of attribution was also made by newspaper editors who reprinted the Dolson story in 1836 and was committed anew by self-styled Alamo expert Michael Lind in the prestigious *Wilson Quarterly* in 1998 as he dared to reopen (but failed to resolve) the case of Crockett's death.[97]

This was not the only judgment made by Dan Kilgore in *How Did Davy Die?* that was independent, unconventional, and dead-on accurate. Walter Lord concluded erroneously in *A Time to Stand* that the de la Peña account of Crockett's death had been published in 1836, and Carmen Perry conceded in 1975 that this might well be true, adding that "if indeed this edition ever appeared, it is possible that most or all copies of it were destroyed because of the highly critical nature of its contents."[98] Scrupulously following the existing evidence, Kilgore stated (p. 15) simply and plainly that the "diary was first published in Mexico in 1955 in the original Spanish."

Subsequent writers would have done well to have taken Dan's conclusion more seriously. Texas bibliographer John H. Jenkins held fast to the myth of an 1836 first edition of the diary when he published *Basic Texas Books* in the 1980s, and in the same decade Crockett scholar Paul Andrew Hutton repeatedly cited the erroneous 1836 publication date even as he defended Kilgore's opinion that Davy had died in captivity rather than in combat.[99] My own research proved in 1994 that Dan was absolutely right about the initial appearance in print of de la Peña's personal narrative of the Texas Revolution.[100]

Why Davy Didn't Die

The decade of the eighties meant the arrival of both the bicentennial of Crockett's birth and the sesquicentennial of his death and thus brought Dan Kilgore back into the limelight at the same time that Paul Andrew Hutton began to establish himself as one of the chief interpreters of Crockett's legacy.[101] By this time, Dan seemed grudgingly reconciled to the inevitability that in the culture at large the mythic hero tales would always overwhelm any mundane effort to set straight the facts of the real man's life.

When asked in 1984 to review Richard Boyd Hauck's *Crockett: A Bio-Bibliography,* Kilgore noted that though the author had recounted "the rather dull facts of the debt-ridden life" of Crockett, "the legend so far outweighs the facts" that most of the writers listed by Hauck "have been motivated by an interest in the mythical Davy rather than the historical David." Kilgore groused that "the public really is not interested in the facts about its hero and would rather not know them."[102] (Dan admitted in a 1993 interview that he had twice tried to sit through the John Wayne cinema version of the fall of the Alamo and had twice failed to make it to the end. It was "too far from reality" for him.)[103]

It was no doubt the impending sesquicentennial of Davy's death at the Alamo that brought Kent Biffle, Texana columnist for the *Dallas Morning News,* to Kilgore's study in January of 1985. Just a few months earlier, Dan had donated most of his collection of books and documents—roughly ten thousand items—to Corpus Christi State University (now Texas A&M University–Corpus Christi), where they became the heart of the Special Collections and Archives division of the Mary and Jeff Bell Library.[104] But Kilgore wasn't quite ready to let go of Davy.

He held on to all of his Crockett materials; they did not come to the university until after Dan's death.[105]

Opening up his scrapbooks in 1985, Kilgore took Biffle on a stroll down memory lane by way of the outraged newspaper commentaries and hate mail that he had accumulated since the publication of *How Did Davy Die?* (though Biffle's subsequent article avoided any mention of the racially tinged castigations that were lurking in some of those letters). Dan told the newspaperman that he had "reached the conclusion that Crockett is today the world's greatest folk hero." Still showing a touch of his frustration with the public's indifference to "the facts" that he had revealed in the Hauck review, Dan also took the opportunity in his conversation with Biffle to make his famous comment that "I wouldn't have minded all this if they'd bought any books. Nobody even read the damn book."[106]

Just a few months later, Kent Biffle would recall Dan's words as the reporter took a much more extensive stroll into the past in the wood-paneled rooms of the DeGolyer Library at Southern Methodist University. He was covering an ambitious attempt to bring together both the facts and the legend of Davy Crockett's death. The occasion was *Alamo Images: Changing Perceptions of a Texas Experience*—the "first major exhibition and companion catalog" to be produced by the DeGolyer Library. The opening symposium, held on November 16, 1985, was titled "Reapproaching the Texas Revolution: The Alamo Myth." Dan himself was nowhere to be seen, but revisionist history was in the air.[107]

When Biffle dropped by the exhibit, Paul Andrew Hutton, the symposium's keynote speaker and the project's "primary advisor," was on hand to show off proudly his own Alamo Play Set, manufactured by the Louis Marx toy company of New York during the Crockett craze of 1955 and now safely protected by one of the DeGolyer's glass cases.[108] Hutton's "extensive collection of popular culture materials" added considerably to the liveliness of the DeGolyer Library's exhibit, noted former director Clifton Jones.[109] The play set was also vivid testimony that Hutton had embraced a doctrine that Kilgore could approach only reluctantly: "The Alamo of the imagination," declared Hutton to one of Biffle's rival reporters from the *Dallas Times Herald,* "is more important than the one of history."[110]

Yet by the mid-1980s Dan certainly could endorse the proposition, put forth in Hutton's introduction to the DeGolyer exhibit's companion catalog, that "there have always been two Alamos—the Alamo of historical fact and the Alamo of our collective imagination."[111] Hutton's pronouncement was approvingly quoted by Kilgore in a new essay of his own, "Why Davy Didn't Die," published in the celebratory anthology *Crockett at Two Hundred: New Perspectives on the Man and the Myth.*[112]

That volume's editors, Tennessee scholars Michael Lofaro and Joe Cummings, brought most of the contributors together for a preliminary bicentennial symposium on August 15, 1986, at East Tennessee State University in Johnson City.[113] Kilgore later recalled with sardonic humor that there were thirty-six people in attendance in the third-floor meeting room, "and twelve or fifteen of us were speakers!"[114] Dan's memory was accurate. A visiting reporter from the *Dallas Times Herald* counted "roughly two dozen people" in the audience who listened to Dan's speech on that day.[115]

Barely twenty miles away, some thirty thousand people were gathering in Limestone, Tennessee, near Crockett's birthplace, to celebrate their hero's two-hundredth anniversary in their own fashion—"buy[ing] the limited-edition bicentennial coonskin caps, watch[ing] men in Davy garb fire muskets[,] and generally revel[ing] in a storied life that most first learned about from a 1950s television series."[116] One visitor from Ohio, when informed that the scholars had some doubts about the legendary Crockett, complained that he didn't "know why they have to mess with Davy so much," and a Crockett descendant took dead aim, metaphorically speaking, at Kilgore's search for the truth through documentary evidence: "It seems someone's always attempting to make a dollar writing negative books about Davy Crockett. They weren't there at the Alamo, so they can't be experts."[117]

Dan took it all in stride. Sporting a "Davy-at-the-Alamo" tie for the occasion in Johnson City, he conceded to David Pasztor of the *Times Herald* that "the average person is not overly concerned with the viewpoints discussed by a few academicians in a remote third-floor university conference room." In that rarified space, reported Pasztor, "men in ties and jackets fumbled with a slide projector and talked about Davy as a 'literary archetype,'" at least once invoking the name of Sigmund Freud.[118]

Dan's mind was not on Freud that day, but on other scholarly pioneers. He took the opportunity provided by the symposium to follow up on a suggestion made back in 1977 by Frank Wardlaw as to how Kilgore might best turn his original presidential address into a book. The Faculty Advisory Committee of Texas A&M University Press felt that Kilgore needed to add an explanation of how the "standard Alamo legend" had made its way into the mainstream historiography of Texas, including not only the popular works by Lon Tinkle and Walter Lord but also the schoolbooks and university texts authored by respected academics.[119]

It's just as well that the committee did not insist on reviewing the expanded manuscript of *How Did Davy Die?* because there were very few additions of this kind in the final version that Kilgore sent to Wardlaw. But now in Tennessee and in his essay for *Crockett at Two Hundred* Dan endeavored to explain just how the "details of the Alamo of our collective imagination" had derived primarily from the writings of two amateur Texas historians, Reuben Marmaduke Potter (1802–90) and William Physick Zuber (1820–1913).[120]

Potter was an American citizen living in Matamoros during the Texas Revolution who later served as a customs agent at Velasco and Galveston during the period of the Texas Republic.[121] He wrote the first historical account of the fall of the Alamo in 1860 and published an extensively revised version of that work in the *Magazine of American History* in 1878. His writings were extremely influential, especially in Texas, where Potter's effort was praised by prominent University of Texas professor Eugene C.

Barker in 1914 as the "most thorough" account of the battle for its time.[122]

Zuber had been a teenaged volunteer soldier in the Texan revolutionary forces but missed both the battle of the Alamo and the alleged visit to his home by a desperate Alamo escapee, Moses Rose. Zuber claimed that Rose had been nursed back to health by Zuber's mother while he regaled her with narrations of the Alamo's (almost) final days, including commander William Barret Travis's now-famous "line in the sand" call for the defenders' ultimate sacrifice. In 1873, almost forty years after the battle, Zuber published his version of the tale that he swore he had learned from his mother.[123]

Zuber's story of the siege of the Alamo was almost immediately incorporated into popular histories and Texas schoolbooks, and the Texan artist Louis Eyth even revised his painting of Travis's last speech to the Alamo garrison in order to include a depiction of the sword-etched line.[124] Reuben M. Potter also had a major influence on the visual imagery that so powerfully shaped the collective Texan imagination when he served as the principal advisor to Henry A. McArdle, whose painting *Dawn at the Alamo* is one of the most frequently reproduced depictions of Crockett's last moments.[125]

I would add to Kilgore's list of influential amateur historians the prolific James T. DeShields (1861–1948), a Texas businessman who in addition to his many historical writings commissioned what is arguably the most famous image of Crockett's final struggle: *The Fall of the Alamo,* or *Crockett's Last Stand.*[126]

85

Painted between 1901 and 1903 by McArdle's crosstown San Antonio rival Robert Jenkins Onderdonk, this classic Texas icon hung for years in DeShields's own Dallas home before finding its way to the Grand Foyer of the Governor's Mansion in Austin. As if still in rivalry with Onderdonk's work for position and influence, McArdle's *Dawn at the Alamo* has hung for most of the past century, along with his matching rendering of the Battle of San Jacinto, on the west wall of the Senate Chamber of the Texas State Capitol.[127]

According to Dan Kilgore, Potter and Zuber were intent most of all to represent the Battle of the Alamo and Crockett's last fight as part of a "great heroic epic."[128] DeShields would certainly have been in hearty agreement. Late in his life he penned an unpublished description of his cherished Onderdonk masterpiece which began with the words, "And they say hero worship comes from the love of freedom!"[129] Both Potter and Zuber, noted Kilgore, "vigorously denounced anyone who questioned that [Crockett] did not die fighting to his last breath," and they took "vehement exception to any suggestion that Crockett died under any other circumstances" than an heroic, last-ditch defense.[130]

Whether or not Dan had captured the full dimensions of the Alamo's place in the "collective imagination," his examination of the influential writings of Zuber and Potter seriously undercut a key claim made by Paul Andrew Hutton at the *Alamo Images* exhibit. Hutton, who had forthrightly stated in his DeGolyer keynote address that "Crockett surrendered and was executed," wrote that not only was "the story of Crockett's surrender quite common in the nineteenth century," but also this version of his death "seemed to upset no one." "Even Theodore Roosevelt," proclaimed Hutton, "included it in his 'Remember the Alamo' story in *Hero Tales from American History*," published in 1895.[131]

Well, not quite. Here is what TR actually wrote about Davy's final scene:

Then . . . the last man stood at bay. It was old Davy Crockett. Wounded in a dozen places, he faced his foes with his back to the wall, ringed around by the bodies of the men he had slain. So desperate was the fight he waged, that the Mexicans who thronged round him were beaten back for the moment, and no one dared to run in upon him. Accordingly, while the lancers held him where he was, for, weakened by wounds and loss of blood, he could not break through them, the musketeers loaded their carbines and shot him down. Santa Anna declined to give him mercy. Some say that when Crockett fell from his wounds, he was taken alive, and was then shot by Santa Anna's order; but his fate cannot be told with certainty, for not a single American was left alive.[132]

The anonymous artist who captured this scene in illustrating Roosevelt's chapter on the Alamo certainly saw no moment of "surrender." Davy is indeed shown facing a line of musketeers with his back against the wall, but he's still holding a pistol in his right hand—hardly a sign of surrender.[133] That TR's own historical imagination included a Crockett surrender is questionable in the extreme.

Hutton has consistently maintained that up until Fess Parker's portrayal of Davy in 1954–55, the story of the surrender and execution "was accepted by most readers [of the Crockett saga] without argument."[134] Dan's reading of Texan historiography led him to a different conclusion. While Kilgore readily acknowledged that "within days after the Alamo's fall, two very different reports of Crockett's final moments were in circulation" (one of the indomitable hero fighting nobly to the bitter end, the other of a captive going down bravely under the sword of the executioner), Dan's reading of Disney's impact was that Fess Parker's Davy *continued,* rather than *created,* the dominance of the legend of Crockett's unyielding stand against impossible odds.[135] My own educated guess is that whether Hutton's generalization was ever valid for the broad sweep of the American republic, Texas was a whole 'nother country, even before Walt Disney's debut as a Crockett biographer.

Dan Kilgore was a careful historian and a cautious reader of texts who seldom if ever allowed his enthusiasms to color his conclusions. Unlike so many, he was never misled by the unproven and undocumented assertions that the de la Peña diary had been published in 1836.[136] Moreover, Kilgore did not hesitate to challenge those who used the S-word. Paul Hutton's chapter in the *Crockett at Two Hundred* anthology immediately followed Dan's chapter and maintained Hutton's unequivocal assertion that Davy had "surrendered." Dan wrote in his own essay that "there is no conclusive evidence that Crockett surrendered."[137] Since both Kilgore and Hutton agreed that the real David Crockett was indeed captured and executed, this last point might turn out to be a matter of semantics, but in matters of fact, Dan's batting average has consistently led the league of Alamo historians.

Yet there was one aspect of the story of Crockett at the Alamo that Paul Hutton could see more clearly, and certainly discuss more forthrightly, than Kilgore: the always controversial issue of *race*. Whether from personal temperament, generational reticence, or his distance from the intellectual trends that were swirling around Hutton in the academic world of the 1980s (Hutton was at the time of the *Alamo Images* exhibit an assistant professor of history at the University of New Mexico), Dan never publicly acknowledged that racial thinking permeated the Texan "creation myth" and the Alamo of the collective imagination, nor that it constituted any part of the outrage aimed at him and his big little book.[138]

Hutton showed no such reticence. The myth of the Alamo, he wrote for the DeGolyer exhibition (notably using the present tense), "is stunningly racist."[139] First of all, Hutton found extensive evidence that Anglo-Texans had come to see in the Alamo their own nineteenth-century Thermopylae, where, as in other mythic battles such as "Custer at the Little Big Horn, and Gordon at Khartoum," there was a consistent cultural message conveyed by these myths:

[T]he heroes are always vastly outnumbered by a vicious enemy from a culturally inferior nation bent on the utter destruction of the heroic band's people. These men fight for their very way of life in a battle that is clearly hopeless. They know that they are doomed but go willingly to their deaths in order to bleed the enemy and buy time for their people.

Oftentimes they are betrayed, sometimes by the failure of their countrymen to rescue them, and usually a lone survivor carries the tale of their sublime fate to the world. They perish with a fierce élan that turns their defeat into a spiritual victory. The leader of the defeated band is often elevated to the status of a national hero, while the battle becomes a point of cultural pride, an example of patriotism and self-sacrifice.[140]

Reuben M. Potter, the first historian of the Alamo, was in San Antonio in 1841 when he saw the first crude Alamo memorial, sculpted out of stones taken from the old mission.[141] Carved on one side was the motto, "Thermopylae had her Messenger of Defeat; but the Alamo had none."[142] The Spartan band of warriors who sacrificed themselves against the Persians at Thermopylae in 480 BCE had, wrote Paul Hutton, bought with their lives time for the other Greeks to rally, "thus insuring the survival of western civilization and the birth of democracy. The Alamo had now matched that ancient struggle, and gone it one better. No one, according to the myth, survived the battle of the Alamo."[143]

Reuben Potter was a man of broad tolerance who maintained strong friendships with Tejanos such as José Antonio Navarro and Juan Seguín and who strongly defended in his historical writings the contributions of Mexican Texans to the cause of the Revolution.[144] Potter was also, as Dan Kilgore argued so persuasively, "committed absolutely to the idea of the Alamo as a great heroic epic" and "remained convinced that Crockett and every other man in the garrison fell fighting at their posts— with the exception of 'a few skulkers.'"[145] According to Kilgore:

"Potter did not justify his views by hard evidence but by his preconceived notion that 'in a fight . . . [when the hopelessly outnumbered] know they have all got to die, the bravest fall first; the last reached is certain to be a sneak. Thus it was at the Alamo. Travis and Crockett fell early on the outworks.' [Potter's] preconceptions [observed Kilgore] required the events to follow a given sequence. Any purported evidence to the contrary would be inconsistent with his theory."[146] To question Davy Crockett's willingness to fight to the last breath would be to fly in the face of what a later generation would call "the power of myth."[147]

But this was not, Paul Hutton insisted, merely a saga of bravery and sacrifice. According to Hutton, "the Alamo story" that served as "a creation myth for Texans" defined a *group identity* that emerged from "a contest of civilizations: freedom vs. tyranny; democracy vs. despotism; Protestantism vs. Catholicism; the New World culture of the United States vs. the Old World culture of Mexico; Anglo-Saxons vs. the mongrelized mixture of Indian and Spanish races, and ultimately, the forces of good over evil."[148] To suggest that Davy Crockett surrendered—or even that he allowed himself to be captured—not only turns him into a "skulker" (to use Potter's term), but also portrays him as willingly yielding to the mongrelized forces of evil.

These were the kind of enemies (depicted in racialized, even bestialized forms by Henry McArdle's *Dawn at the Alamo*) to whom a hero of Crockett's caliber (and race) would never surrender. Art historian Emily F. Cutrer describes McArdle's "Manichean vision of the combatants" embodied by the dark

91

and "apelike" Mexican soldier locked in combat with a Davy Crockett whose whiteness and noble bearing are highlighted by the artist's technique. Referring directly to the detail from the painting that ironically was chosen for the cover of *How Did Davy Die?* Cutrer asserts that "Crockett and the Mexican are not merely two men, they are two races that represent opposing forces in the painter's mind."[149]

Without casting aspersions on either Reuben M. Potter or William P. Zuber, it is fair to say that in the late nineteenth and early twentieth centuries there was in the United States what Cecilia Elizabeth O'Leary has called a "racialization of patriotism," in which the definition of Americanism became virtually equated with "whiteness."[150] Historian David Blight has shown that by the turn of the century, ritual remembrances of the Civil War, at the same time that they celebrated brotherhood and reconciliation between Union and Confederate veterans, had virtually erased the role of African American troops in the war, and had reduced the status of blacks at commemorative events to that of lackeys and groundskeepers, if their presence was allowed at all.[151]

In Texas, a corresponding process was taking place with regard to citizens of Mexican descent. Historian David Montejano has shown that "by the early twentieth century, the story of the Alamo and Texas frontier history had become purged of its ambiguities—of the fact that Mexicans and Anglos had often fought on the same side."[152] In the binary mythic structure described above by Hutton's "contest of civilizations," one was either a "Mexican" or a "Texan." There was no complex middle ground where darker-skinned, Spanish-speaking Catholic men of Mexican birth fought for the same freedom from tyranny as did Davy Crockett. Tejano revolutionaries such as José Antonio Navarro or Juan Seguín were erased from popular memories of the Texan past just as surely as they were absent from the canvases of Henry McArdle and Robert Onderdonk.[153]

With "historical lessons" being taken from a mythicized past rather than from what Kilgore called "hard evidence," Texas history, argues David Montejano, was being used to define and rationalize "the proper place of [the Mexicans as] a colored people." Segregation and disfranchisement policies were being carried out in Texas as well as in many other Southern states, and "Texan historical memories played a part similar to Reconstruction memories in the Jim Crow South" in justifying these measures.[154]

Even in the late twentieth century, after explicit segregation laws (which had affected Mexican Americans as well as African Americans in Texas) had been dismantled, anthropologists Holly Brear and Richard Flores, in their separate examinations of the "lessons" that have been taught to pilgrims visiting the Alamo historic site, each found rigid hierarchies of racial identity encoded in the structure of the legends, rituals, and public spaces surrounding this Texas shrine. They agree that there has been a pernicious "binary logic" at work in the depiction of a conflict between noble Anglos and "treacherous Mexicans," with unfortunate effects on the perspectives of the observers.[155]

What kinds of unfortunate effects? When Richard Flores was himself a San Antonio third-grader, his class made a field trip to the Alamo. As the students emerged into the bright sunlight, his best friend (an Anglo) whispered to him, "You killed them. You and the other 'mes'kins'!"[156] Historian Andrés Tijerina received a more public shaming in his West Texas classroom. After his Anglo teacher had finished presenting the history of the Alamo battle, she pointed to the ten-year-old and said, "It was your grandfather, Andrés, who killed Davy Crockett!"[157]

At least he got to stay in the room. A former university president in Texas tells of the time in the 1950s when his seventh-grade Texas history teacher began her lecture on the Battle of the Alamo by sending the two Hispanic students in the class out of the room "because they were not worthy to hear this heroic tale."[158] Publishing executive Anastasio Bueno told cultural scholar Edward Linenthal in the late 1980s that "we learned in the third or fourth grade that we killed the Alamo heroes." Ray Sanchez, a former dean at San Antonio College, "added that most of his Mexican American friends were ashamed that 'they killed Davy Crockett.'"[159]

The hierarchical understanding of racial and ethnic status in Texas went beyond the casual shaming of Tejano children to "put them in their place." One telling example comes from the Kilgore files at Texas A&M University Press. Frank Wardlaw had sent a copy of *How Did Davy Die?* to Joe B. Frantz, the director of the Texas State Historical Association. In his reply Frantz commented on the huge response to Dan's book—negative as well as positive—that was all over the newspapers and radio in the week following its publication. Frantz went on to say: "Oh, well, maybe it will get the Daughters of the Republic of Texas [the caretakers of the Alamo] on Dan's back and off mine. They have never forgiven me for naming a Mexican American to a Clara Driscoll scholarship."[160]

Dan Kilgore should have known in 1978 that he was setting out to revise the collective imagination as well as to settle a historical dispute when he wrote *How Did Davy Die?* As Frantz told Wardlaw, "A non-professional historian is going to wind up revising all our notions about the Alamo and the men who fought there."[161] But Kilgore may not have realized that he was stirring up a more powerful witches' brew of dark and powerful feelings. Historian Fitzhugh Brundage notes that "any attempt to revise the public memory almost inevitably compels a revision of existing hierarchies, whether they relate to race, class, gender, ethnicity, or religion."[162] Where there is this kind of revision, there is always resistance.

Moreover, Kilgore may not have fully recognized, as Paul Hutton certainly did, the crucial connection between historical myth and a strongly felt sense of *identity*—both group and personal—that modern scholars of "public memory" have found operating in virtually all societies.[163] At the *Alamo Images* exhibit, Hutton told Kent Biffle: "The symbolic power of the Alamo nears the religious in many people's minds. Any attempt to tamper with the Alamo of the imagination will be resisted by staunch defenders of the true faith. To suggest that Davy Crockett surrendered [a word that Kilgore, of course, had avoided] is to attack a symbol that people embrace as a part of their self-identification."[164]

Brundage writes: "So tightly bound together are collective memory and self-identification that memory is the thread of personal identity. . . . When appealing to a collective memory, individuals necessarily define themselves in relation to inherited conventions and hierarchies."[165]

It is important at this point to stress that not all critics of the hypothesis of Crockett's execution in captivity were motivated by ethnic identities or racial agendas. Just as Reuben Potter could argue his case with a defense of Crockett's heroism and bravery rather than his race, so could critics of Kilgore such as Bill Groneman approach the task in the spirit of a defense of the heroic Crockett legend. This is precisely what Groneman did in his 1994 book, *Defense of a Legend: Crockett and the de la Peña Diary,* but he did so knowing that racial arguments and counterarguments had sometimes poisoned what both Kilgore and Groneman had hoped could be a discussion of documentary evidence. "The not-too-subtle message was sent out," complained Groneman, "that if you did not believe the de la Peña account, then you were a racist."[166]

Bill was not simply being paranoid. Using Kilgore's analysis of Reuben Potter's flawed methodology as a point of departure, anthropologist Richard Flores has argued that "the erasure of the historical Crockett by Potter and others in favor of the legendary Davy coincides with efforts nationwide to rewrite the past in the spirit of nationalism, patriotism, and valor. But here

patriotism works to enforce a racial hierarchy and class formation that privileges a few. . . . In effect, the heroic Davy is made
in the image of the new American patriot whose valor reproduces
the nation and whose death purifies the polis from those whose
racial formation or cultural heritage darkens the American land-
scape."[167] Moreover, Flores argued that the Crockett craze of Fess
Parker and John Wayne (whose 1960 movie *The Alamo* was cast
in an equally heroic vein) cannot be separated from the political
realities of the 1950s, a time when demands for equality by black
and Hispanic Americans were being shouted down by those accusing the protesters of being Communists and subversives.
"[T]his new wave of Crockett patriotism," Flores maintains,
"was an effort to divert attention from issues of inequality and
racial injustice."[168] Such charges, easy to make in broad cultural
terms, become harder to justify without direct evidence when
they are leveled at individual researchers, historians, and advo-
cates. There is no such evidence with regard to Reuben Potter, or
for that matter to Bill Groneman.

Dan Kilgore had to be as aware of the anti-Mexican racial
comments in the hostile letters he received as he was of their accusations that he was a communist and a smut peddler. He chose to
ridicule the latter openly but to smother with silence the former.[169]
Perhaps, in his South Texas of the 1970s (this was the decade of the
controversial Raza Unida Party, which for a time governed Crystal
City and Zavala County), it was just too sore a subject.[170] Kilgore's
alleged communism could be laughed at in Corpus Christi; rac-
ism and ethnic conflict were too serious to be joking matters.

Dan retired from his accounting firm in 1986, and he received his last royalty check for *How Did Davy Die?*—for twenty-three dollars and ninety-one cents—in 1990.[171] Throughout the decade of the 1980s, Bill Groneman was crafting an ever more impressive argument that there was something very fishy about the de la Peña diary. In 1993 he submitted to the *Southwestern Historical Quarterly* an article arguing that the manuscript was a probable forgery, and the editor of the journal, George Ward, sent the Groneman submission to Kilgore for his comments.[172]

Dan responded to Ward that he could "find no reason that it should not be published." He noted that Groneman "has criticized me several times as a revisionist but I won't hold that against him."[173] Actually, Groneman offered almost no criticism of Kilgore in the proposed article, but rather concentrated his fire on what he (with some justification) deemed to be misleading editorial lapses in the English translation of the memoir, *With Santa Anna in Texas.*[174] This, no doubt, is why Dan added the following note to George Ward at the end of his letter: "Carmen Perry agonized greatly over the criticism she got over the translation. This will shake her up."[175]

Dan was somewhat shaken himself by the series of anomalies that Bill Groneman had discovered in the English translation, in the 1955 Mexican publication of *La Rebelión de Texas,* and in the original de la Peña manuscripts, held at the time by Special Collections in the John Peace Library at the University of Texas at San Antonio. The *Southwestern Historical Quarterly* reported that at the March 1994 TSHA meeting in Austin, "Dan

Kilgore himself admitted that Groneman is probably right about the diary being a fake."[176]

That meeting of the TSHA was the first one that I had attended since 1986, and only my second TSHA meeting since 1977. I regret that in that earlier year I was young and foolish (and poor), and did not buy a ticket to hear Dan's presidential speech about how Davy had died. The 1994 meeting was a more auspicious one for me. I received the H. Bailey Carroll Award for my recent article proving that Sam Houston had not actually given a bitterly racist speech attributed to him by most twentieth-century authorities.[177]

After the meeting, I traveled to San Antonio to look at some Republic of Texas manuscripts held by the DRT Library at the Alamo. Davy Crockett was not on my mind. I had seen a notice of Bill Groneman's forthcoming *Defense of a Legend*, but when *Quarterly* editor George Ward had asked me in Austin if I had seen it, I had to admit that I had been too busy with my own work on Sam Houston and Juan Seguín over the preceding year to have paid much attention to the rekindled Crockett controversy. Little did I know that I was about to be swept up in this very vortex—and that (at least up to the present time) I would never miss another TSHA meeting.

A harbinger of my future relationship with Dan Kilgore and Davy Crockett came on my first day in San Antonio, when Bill Groneman walked into the DRT Library. It's a small place, and I couldn't help overhearing his conversation as he introduced himself to the attendant. I immediately introduced myself to

Bill, and we two historical detectives plunged into a discussion of our recent work. Just as soon as the library closed, I hustled over to the nearby bookstore where Bill was signing copies of *Defense of a Legend,* and happily left with my new copy in hand, duly signed by both Groneman and his cover illustrator, Don Griffiths.

Back in North Carolina I put the book on the top of my stack of anticipated summer reading, but a call from George Ward replaced temptation with obligation when he asked me to review *Defense of a Legend* for the *Southwestern Historical Quarterly.* What I expected to be a one- or two-page favorable review (after all, Bill had even included a photograph of the alleged forger of the de la Peña diary) turned into a forty-page refutation—an argument for the authenticity of the de la Peña manuscripts and a full-blown confirmation of Kilgore's basic conclusions in *How Did Davy Die?* I had been fortunate enough to discover, using finding aids that were unavailable to Dan in the 1970s, a one-of-a-kind, previously unknown pamphlet that José Enrique de la Peña had written from prison in 1839. It contained sufficient evidence to lay to rest Groneman's most serious charges against the memoir of the Mexican soldier.[178]

The next year's trip to the TSHA meeting in San Antonio was surreal. Both Groneman's talk before a standing-room-only crowd and my rebuttal of his thesis later the same day before the Alamo Battlefield Association were covered by both *Texas Monthly* and documentary filmmaker Brian Huberman.[179] As a result of my alleged "attacks" on Crockett's heroism, I was in-

100

troduced at cocktail parties as "The Anti-Christ," and a woman who recognized me on the street after seeing me ask Bill Groneman a question at his TSHA session called out to me that she'd like to "gut you right now with a Bowie knife, because hanging would be too good for you!" But it wasn't all negative. In a memorable moment at the TSHA book exhibits, someone tapped me on the shoulder. When I turned around, a smiling Dan Kilgore said, "I'd like to shake your hand."

This was my first and last meeting with Dan. We exchanged a couple of letters, but just before Christmas, Dan passed away. By that time I was beginning to get my own hate mail, and I was somewhat surprised by the explicit anti-Mexican sentiments it contained. Having caught up by this time on the discussions of Dan's mail by both Kent Biffle and Paul Hutton, neither of whom had mentioned such content, I was puzzled for several reasons.[180] First, was I the only one receiving such responses? Second, why were these people who were so angry at Mexicans also mad at me, since I was essentially arguing that the Mexican army had killed Crockett in cold blood? Most importantly, what was the deeper significance of such a response to the story of Davy's capture and execution?

In the course of trying to answer these questions, I was led by a hunch to Corpus Christi, where Tom Kreneck and Carol Kilgore graciously made available to me the still-uncataloged boxes of Dan's papers most recently acquired by Special Collections at the Bell Library. In those boxes in the summer of 1998 I found what I was looking for, and I began my effort to weave together what I was learning about racial invective, popular culture, collective memory, and the documentary evidence from the nineteenth century. The results were a book, several articles, and a memorable trip to Tuscany, where I presented to an international conference the somewhat pretentiously titled paper, "Why 'How He Died' Became 'Who We Are': The Texan Identity and the Contested Iconography of Davy Crockett's Death at the Alamo."[181]

In the meantime, I carried on several running battles in historical journals with Bill Groneman and his colleague Thomas Ricks Lindley (who tragically suffered an untimely death in 2007).[182] I have learned much from these exchanges with Bill and Tom, but nothing that I have learned has led me to doubt that Dan Kilgore got it right. Subsequent scholarship has confirmed, and not overturned, what he concluded when he put his impressive analytical skills to work over thirty years ago on the question of just how Davy died.

When Texas A&M University Press asked me to write a substantial afterword to a thirtieth-anniversary reissue of *How Did Davy Die?* I jumped at the chance, despite other obligations. I regret that those obligations prevented me from completing this retrospective on Dan and his work in time for the 2008 anniversary, but I have absolutely no regrets about spending more time with Dan Kilgore. When I met Carol Kilgore for a delicious seafood dinner in Corpus Christi upon the completion of my second foray into the Kilgore Collection in March of 2008, I may have startled her by telling her that I had just spent the past three days with Dan.

She quickly realized what I meant when I referred to my recent total immersion into her beloved husband's papers. The personality that emerges from those scribbles, notes, chapters, clippings, brickbats, and accolades is one deserving of enormous respect. Dan was a good, thoughtful, honest man. He was an amateur in the best sense of that word: he loved history, and he gave it his best. And his best was very, very good.

Notes to "Dan Kilgore and His Big Little Book"

1. Undated "Book Notes" page (77) from the *Journal of the East Texas Historical Association*, from the back files of Texas A&M University Press, courtesy Editor-in-chief Mary Lenn Dixon (hereinafter cited as A&M Press Back Files).

2. Shaun Usher, "Davy Crockett Dies Again," *Daily Mail* (London), April 28, 1978, clipping in Dan E. Kilgore Collection, Special Collections and Archives, Mary and Jeff Bell Library, Texas A&M University at Corpus Christi (hereinafter cited as Kilgore Collection). I am deeply grateful to Special Collections Director Thomas H. Kreneck and Archivist Grace Charles for their kind responses to my multiple requests for their assistance over the past decade.

3. Thomas H. Kreneck, "Dan Kilgore: 'Demon Collector' and Texas History Benefactor," in *Collecting Texas: Essays on Texana Collectors and the Creation of Research Libraries,* ed. Thomas H. Kreneck and Gerald D. Saxon (Dallas: Book Club of Texas, forthcoming), 171; see also Thomas H. Kreneck, "Dan Kilgore and *How Did Davy Die?*" unpublished manuscript presented at the conference "Eyewitness to the Texas Revolution: José Enrique de la Peña and His Narrative," Austin, Texas, April 29, 2000, 2. Kilgore told an interviewer in 1993 that he considered his book "a simple historical exercise" in the use of sources to come to a conclusion. Thanks to Brian Huberman of Rice University for providing a videotaped copy of his complete interview with Kilgore, (hereinafter cited as Huberman/Kilgore video interview).

4. "Take That, John Wayne," *Texas Monthly,* August 1978, 78.

5. Paul Andrew Hutton, "Introduction," in *A Narrative of the Life of David Crockett of the State of Tennessee, Written by Himself* (Lincoln and London: University of Nebraska Press, 1987), xli–xliii.

6. Paul Andrew Hutton, "Davy Crockett, Still King of the Wild Frontier: And a Hell of a Nice Guy Besides," *Texas Monthly,* November 1986, 248. For an interpretive analysis of the Davy Crockett craze, see Margaret J. King, "The Recycled Hero: Walt Disney's Davy Crockett," in *Davy Crockett: The Man, the Legend, the Legacy, 1786–1986,* ed. Michael A. Lofaro (Knoxville, University of Tennessee Press, 1985), 137–58.

7. Carol Kilgore quoted in Bob Tutt, "Crockett's Death Mystery Lives On," *Houston Chronicle,* Section E, March 8, 1998.

8. José Enrique de la Peña, *La Rebelión de Texas: Manuscrito Inédito de 1836 por un Oficial de Santa Anna,* ed. J. Sánchez Garza (Mexico City: A. Frank de Sánchez, 1955), iv, 70. For a discussion of the distinction between the diary and the memoir in the de la Peña manuscripts, see James E. Crisp, "Introduction," in José Enrique de la Peña, *With Santa Anna in Texas: A Personal Narrative of the Revolution,* trans. and ed. Carmen Perry, expanded edition (College Station: Texas A&M University Press, 1997), xxii–xxiv.

9. Lon Tinkle, *13 Days to Glory: The Siege of the Alamo* (New York: McGraw-Hill Book Co., 1958; reprint, College Station: Texas A&M University Press, 1996), 213–14, 248.

10. Walter Lord, *A Time to Stand: The Epic of the Alamo* (1961; reprint, Lincoln and London: University of Nebraska Press, 1978), 174–75, 198, 206–207.

11. John Lumpkin, "Did Santa Anna 'Execute' Crockett?" *San Antonio Light,* September 9, 1975; Vickie Davidson, "Diary Says Crockett Died by Execution," *San Antonio Express,* September 10, 1975.

12. See two documents written by Susan Jacobson located in the Carmen Perry file at the DRT Library at the Alamo: the first is "Uproar in Texas," the original typescript of an article intended for *People* magazine; the second is "Biographical Information on Carmen Perry from Susan Jacobson." The article ultimately appeared, heavily edited and without Jacobson's by-line, under the misleading title "Did Crockett Die at the Alamo? Historian Carmen Perry Says No," in the September 26, 1975, issue of *People* magazine. See also Susan Jacobson's apologetic letter to Carmen Perry, May 23, 1976, in the same file at the DRT Library.

13. Eve Lynn Sawyer, "Crockett Furor Simmers," *San Antonio Express-News,* October 26, 1975; Robert Elder, Jr., "For John Peace III, Finally a Chance to Forget the Alamo," *Wall Street Journal,* "Texas Journal" Section, September 2, 1998, pp. T1, T4. The statement about the "old papers" in the suitcase was made by John Peace III, speaking in *The De la Peña Diary,* a video documentary produced by Brian Huberman, Edward Hugetz, and Cynthia Ann Lost Howling Wolf (Houston: BH Films, 2000).

14. Lynwood Abram, "Frank Wardlaw Ending Career at A&M Press," *Houston Chronicle,* "People" Section, February 19, 1978; "A&M Enters Publishing Field," undated clipping from the *Eagle Lake Post,* Carmen Perry scrapbooks in the private collection of Carmen Perry's nephew, Robert Perry, Austin, Texas. Copies of many of these items may also be found in the Car-

men Perry scrapbooks (1975–77) and vertical file in the Daughters of the Republic of Texas Library. I am grateful to Robert Perry for providing copies of the scrapbooks and correspondence. See José Enrique de la Peña, *With Santa Anna in Texas: A Personal Narrative of the Revolution,* trans. and ed. Carmen Perry, 1st ed. (College Station: Texas A&M University Press, 1975).

15. "Author Receives Award for Book," *San Antonio Express,* April 4, 1976; "The Alamo: Book Fires New Battle," *The Discourse* (University of Texas at San Antonio) 4, no. 5 (May 1976).

16. See above, note 12.

17. Charlotte Phelan, "The Davy Crockett Affray," *Houston Post,* April 4, 1976.

18. Carmen Perry to Dan Kilgore, March 14, 1977, Kilgore Collection. On the Bum Steer Award, see Kent Biffle, "Surrender? Davy's Fans Never Will," *Dallas Morning News,* January 13, 1985.

19. Phelan, "Davy Crockett Affray."

20. Kreneck, "Dan Kilgore and *How Did Davy Die?*" 2.

21. See above, note 3.

22. Kreneck, "Dan Kilgore: 'Demon Collector,'" 163; Linda Carrico, "CCSU Gets Kilgore Texas History Collection," *Corpus Christi Caller-Times,* August 27, 1984; Vivienne Heines, "Prominent Local Historian and Accountant Kilgore Dies at 74," *Corpus Christi Caller-Times,* December 24, 1995.

23. Kreneck, "Dan Kilgore: 'Demon Collector,'" 164.

24. Ibid., 169.

25. "Historian Just Wants the Facts," *Houston Chronicle,* June 11, 1961.

26. D. E. Kilgore, *A Ranger Legacy: 150 Years of Service to Texas* (Austin: Madrona Press, 1973), text from dust jacket in Kilgore biographical file, Center for American History, University of Texas at Austin.

27. J. Hefter (Mexico City) to D. E. Kilgore, October 30, 1967, Kilgore Collection; Dan Kilgore to the Library of Congress, October 19, 1968, Kilgore Collection.

28. See the copy of the typescript, already bearing the final title, as well as the letter of March 10, 1977, from Kilgore to Frank Wardlaw, both in the Kilgore Collection.

29. James M. Day, "How Did Davy Die?" *El Paso Times,* July 23, 1978, Kilgore Collection. An undated "Book Notes" clipping from the *Journal of the East Texas Historical Association* (A&M Press Back Files; see note 1, above) called the Dallas address "well received."

30. Carmen Perry to Mr. Kilgore, March 14, 1977, Kilgore Collection.

31. Kreneck, "Dan Kilgore: 'Demon Collector,'" 171. Kilgore mentions the Baker Hotel event in the 1993 Huberman/Kilgore video interview.

32. Dan Kilgore to Frank Wardlaw, October 30, 1977, Kilgore Collection.

33. Statement by Kilgore (in the first person) in the 1993 Huberman/Kilgore video interview.

34. Press release from the Texas A&M University News Service, drafted April 20, 1978, by "Stephenson," A&M Press Back Files; copy of identical press release marked "Received: TAMRF, April 21, 1978," Kilgore Collection.

35. Statements by Kilgore in the 1993 Huberman/Kilgore video interview; April 21 entry "Cactus Prior [*sic*]" for appointments calendar for 1978, Kilgore Collection.

36. Lamont Wood, "Was Alamo Hero Executed?" *San Antonio Light,* April 22, 1978.

37. Ibid.

38. Dan Kilgore, "Working Copy," Kilgore Collection, 13. This quotation comes from several pages of the original text that were dropped by the editors from the published version of Dan Kilgore, "Why Davy Didn't Die," in *Crockett at Two Hundred: New Perspectives on the Man and the Myth,* ed. Michael A. Lofaro and Joe Cummings (Knoxville: University of Tennessee Press, 1989), 7–19. For a discussion of the editing of Kilgore's text, see Joe Cummings to Dan Kilgore, October 10, 1987, Kilgore Collection.

39. Press release, April 20, 1978, A&M Press Back Files, 1; "Historian Shatters Crockett Legend," *Bryan–College Station Eagle,* April 21, 1978; "'How Did Davy Die?' History Buff Claims Crockett No Hero," *Houston Post,* April 22, 1978. Kilgore claimed that the complete version of the rewritten release from the AP added "Willie Nelson albums" to the lizard-skin cowboy boots, but the editors in Houston and College Station, at least, used their editorial discretion to remove the albums, though they kept the boots. See Kilgore, "Working Copy," Kilgore Collection, 14. Kilgore told Brian Huberman in his videotaped interview that the AP rewrite man had "worked [the release] over," but news stories based on the AP wire story largely followed the original press release, verbatim, after the first few sentences.

40. Press release, April 20, 1978, A&M Press Back Files, 1–3.

41. Jackie Hardy to "Dan Kilgore—accountant," April 22, 1978, Kilgore Collection.

42. Bill Walraven, "Second Battle of the Alamo Looms: Report Davy Crockett Captured Provokes Angry Outcry," *Corpus Christi Caller,* May 2, 1978.

43. Frank Wardlaw to Jean Andrews, May 3, 1978, A&M Press Back Files.

44. Kilgore's good friend Bill Walraven concluded (without mentioning Knaggs's name) in his May 8, 1978, column in the *Corpus Christi Caller* that Knaggs had not read *How Did Davy Die?* "I figure if the author is good on research," wrote Walraven, "he ought to read a book before he knocks it in print." See also *The Bugles Are Silent: A Novel of the Texas Revolution* (Austin: Shoal Creek Publishers, 1977).

45. "Crockett's Integrity Upheld in New Book," *The Austin Citizen,* April 28, 1978.

46. "Remember the Alamo, but Forget Crockett Surrender, Author Says," *Dallas Morning News,* April 28, 1978; Shoal Creek Publishers "News Release," April 28, 1978.

47. Dan [Kilgore] to Frank [Wardlaw], June 24, 1978, A&M Press Back Files.

48. Dan Kilgore to Mr. Wade, June 22, 1978, manuscript copy on notebook paper, Kilgore Collection. For Knaggs's UPI affiliation, see the dust jacket for *The Bugles Are Silent,* Kilgore Collection.

49. [Dan Kilgore], "Sources," handwritten notes on ledger paper, Kilgore Collection, 4.

50. Without mentioning their names, Kilgore made it clear that he was still mightily irked at both Knaggs and Simon in a 1986 interview with *Texas Monthly.* See Barbara Paulsen, "Say It Ain't So, Davy," *Texas Monthly,* November 1986, 129. Kilgore's quotes from Simon are accurate. See Roger Simon, "Davy Crockett was a Flop? You Gotta Be Kiddin,'" *Denver Post,* June 11, 1978. Dan's reference to the fifteen-minute interview may be found on page 3 of his handwritten "Sources," Kilgore Collection.

51. Roger Simon, "Writer Who Slurred Crockett Starts Getting Some Hate Mail," *Houston Chronicle,* May 7, 1978.

52. Carmen Perry to Mr. Kilgore, May 1, 1978, Kilgore Collection (original emphasis).

53. Jackie Hardy to "Dan Kilgore—accountant," April 22, 1978, Kilgore Collection.

54. Roger Simon, "Davy Crockett was a Flop?"

55. Dan [Kilgore] to Frank [Wardlaw], June 24, 1978, A&M Press Back Files.

56. Statement by Kilgore in the 1993 Huberman/Kilgore video interview.

57. Frank M. Dyer to Mr. Dan E. Kilgore, postmarked May 10, 1978,

Kilgore Collection. The original five-dollar price of *How Did Davy Die?* was reported in Kent Biffle, "Surrender? Davy's Fans Never Will," *Dallas Morning News,* January 13, 1985.

58. Frank M. Dyer to Mr. Dan E. Kilgore, postmarked May 10, 1978, Kilgore Collection.

59. T. Harris, "Statements on Crockett Were Part of a Pattern," letter to editor, *Houston Chronicle,* May 17, 1978.

60. O. Uzzell to [Dan Kilgore], Fort Myers, Fla., May 23, 1978, Kilgore Collection.

61. The only notice that Kilgore ever seems to have given to the racial theme struck by some of his critics came in a private, tongue-in-cheek letter that he sent to Frank Wardlaw upon the latter's announced retirement from Texas A&M University Press for reasons of health. Less than two weeks after the appearance of the bitter letter from T. Harris in the *Houston Chronicle,* Kilgore told Wardlaw that while his "double bypass job" might lend "credibility to your excuse . . . , we with perception to understand the plot to defame white American heroes are aware of the true reason for your untimely departure." Dan also thanked Wardlaw for having given him the opportunity to receive "the accolades of being a communist as well as a mealy-mouth, intellectual CPA, obsessed with a craving to be controversial. And nice offers to have my eyes plucked out and my mouth washed out with soap." D. E. Kilgore to Frank [Wardlaw], May 30, 1978, Kilgore Collection. See also Abram, "Frank Wardlaw Ending Career at A&M Press."

The reference to having his eyes plucked out was based on a short editorial about Kilgore's little book that had appeared in the *Austin American-Statesman* on April 25. It quoted Ambrose Bierce's definition of a cynic as "a blackguard whose faulty vision sees things as they are, not as they ought to be. Hence the custom among the Scythians of plucking out a cynic's eyes to improve his vision."

62. Dan [Kilgore] to Frank [Wardlaw], June 24, 1978, A&M Press Back Files.

63. Llerena Friend, "Historical Detective's Work," *Wichita Falls Times,* Sunday Magazine, May 14, 1978, 22. See also Llerena Friend, "Introduction," in de la Peña, *With Santa Anna in Texas,* 1975 edition, xv–xxiii.

64. See the following reviews of *How Did Davy Die?:* Gene Brack, *Southwestern Historical Quarterly* 82 (April 1979): 467–68; David L. Coon, *Chronicles of Oklahoma* 57 (Summer 1979): 238–39; Emmett M. Essin, *Tennessee Historical Quarterly* 38 (Winter 1979): 505–506. Perry's translation was reviewed in the *American Historical Review,* the *Pacific Historical Review,* the

Journal of Southern History, the *Journal of the West, American West, Arizona and the West*, the *New Mexico Historical Review*, and the *Chronicles of Oklahoma*.

65. Kilgore, quoted in Biffle, "Surrender? Davy's Fans Never Will."

66. The quoted words are those of Paul Andrew Hutton from his "Introduction" in Susan Prendergast Schoelwer with Tom W. Gläser, *Alamo Images: Changing Perceptions of a Texas Experience* (Dallas: DeGolyer Library and Southern Methodist University Press, 1985), 3. See pp. 16–17 for Hutton's description of the popular response to *How Did Davy Die?*

67. Bill Groneman, "Crockett's Last Stand," *Alamo Lore and Myth Organization* Newsletter 4, issue 4 (December 1982): 1.

68. Bill Groneman, *Defense of a Legend: Crockett and the de la Peña Diary* (Plano: Republic of Texas Press, 1994), ix.

69. *Wilson Quarterly* 22, no. 1 (Winter 1998): contents page. Michael Lind's article on "The Death of David Crockett" in this issue of the *WQ* (pp. 50–57) touched off its own little skirmish, with both Bill Groneman and myself taking part. The Lind article and the ensuing exchanges have been archived online at http://www.tamu.edu/ccbn/dewitt/adp/archives/delapena/lind_crisp/lind.html.

70. Groneman, "Crockett's Last Stand," 1.

71. See the review of *How Did Davy Die?* by Gene Brack, *Southwestern Historical Quarterly* 82 (April 1979): 468.

72. Walraven, "Second Battle of the Alamo Looms" (my emphasis).

73. "Take That, John Wayne," 78.

74. Statement by Kilgore in the 1993 Huberman/Kilgore video interview.

75. "Take That, John Wayne," 78.

76. Bill Groneman, one of the chief critics of Kilgore's thesis, refers to Ramón Martínez Caro as "the only verifiable Mexican eyewitness to the [Alamo] executions." See Groneman, *Defense of a Legend*, 51.

77. Groneman, "Crockett's Last Stand," 5–6.

78. Ibid., 5.

79. Ibid., 6.

80. Ibid., 7. Groneman's argument was incorporated into a later book that he coauthored with Phil Rosenthal. See their *Roll Call at the Alamo* (Fort Collins, Colo.: Old Army Press, 1985), 29–37. The reader of the complete accounts by Núñez and Soldana may disagree with Groneman's claim that they are without "embellishments." Moreover, given Groneman's criticism of Kilgore's "accounting" approach to his sources, it is interesting to note that in advertising *Roll Call at the Alamo* the Old Army Press claimed the following:

"Citing fully as many contemporary accounts as Kilgore, Bill [Groneman] ably defends the popular picture of the legendary frontiersman's death." As we have seen with regard to the issue of immediacy, the word "contemporary" is used loosely here. See the four-page flyer from the Old Army Press featuring *Roll Call at the Alamo* as volume 1 of the "Source Texana Series" addressed to Dan Kilgore, Kilgore Collection.

81. See Kilgore, *How Did Davy Die?* 26; Kilgore subsequently established that the Becerra recollections were first published by John S. "Rip" Ford in *Albert Hanford's Texas State Register for 1878* (Galveston: A. Hanford, 1878), 30. See Francisco Becerra, *A Mexican Sergeant's Recollections of the Alamo and San Jacinto,* as told to John S. Ford in 1875, with introduction by Dan Kilgore (Austin: Jenkins Publishing Company, 1980), 13.

82. Stephen L. Hardin, "The Félix Núñez Account and the Siege of the Alamo: A Critical Appraisal," *Southwestern Historical Quarterly* 94, no. 1 (July 1990): 72.

83. Ibid., 70.

84. James T. DeShields, *Tall Men with Long Rifles* (San Antonio: The Naylor Company, 1935; reprint, 1971), 183. The words "Set Down and Written Out by James T. DeShields as told to him by Creed Taylor" are to be found on the title page of this book but are at best misleading and more likely a lie.

85. Jack Jackson and James E. Ivey, "Mystery Artist of the Alamo: José Juan Sánchez," *Southwestern Historical Quarterly* 105, no. 2 (October 2001): 241, note 95. See also Stephen L. Hardin, *Texian Iliad: A Military History of the Texas Revolution* (Austin: University of Texas Press, 1994), 281, note 3. The original manuscript of the "John W. Hunter Literary Effort," which is based on Hunter's interviews of Creed Taylor, is housed in the Archives Division of the Texas State Library, Austin.

86. Groneman, *Defense of a Legend,* 95–98, 101–103; Jackson and Ivey, "Mystery Artist of the Alamo," 238–44 (especially p. 241). Though Kilgore (*How Did Davy Die?* 38) cited only editions of the Sánchez Navarro journal published in the 1960s, its first publication was in 1938. See Carlos Sánchez-Navarro, ed., *La Guerra de Tejas: Memorias de un Soldado* (Mexico City: Editorial Polis, 1938).

87. See above, note 8.

88. See Don Carleton, "Post-Mortem of a Hero," *Texas Magazine* supplement to the *Houston Chronicle,* June 25, 2000, 8–12.

89. See Thomas Lawrence Connelly, ed., "Did David Crockett Surrender at the Alamo? A Contemporary Letter," *Journal of Southern History* 36

(August 1960): 368–76, and "Contributors," 438. (Dan Kilgore misspelled the name as "Conelly.") See also Lord, *A Time to Stand,* 206. Lord repeated his mistaken identification of Dolson's informant as Almonte in Walter Lord, "Myths and Realities of the Alamo," in Stephen B. Oates, ed., *The Republic of Texas* (Palo Alto, Calif.: *American West* Magazine and the Texas State Historical Association, 1968), 24.

90. See Ramón Martínez Caro, "A True Account of the First Texas Campaign and the Events Subsequent to the Battle of San Jacinto," in Carlos E. Castañeda, trans., *The Mexican Side of the Texan Revolution* (Dallas: P. L. Turner Company, 1928), 123–42. See also James E. Crisp, "Documenting Davy's Death: The Problematic 'Dolson Letter' from Texas, 1836," *Journal of the West* 46, no. 2 (Spring 2007): 22–28; and Margaret Swett Henson, "Politics and the Treatment of the Mexican Prisoners after the Battle of San Jacinto," *Southwestern Historical Quarterly* 94, no. 2 (October 1990): 188–230.

91. For the Dolson Letter, see Crisp, "Documenting Davy's Death," 24; Connelly, "Did David Crockett Surrender?" 373–74. For Martínez Caro's account, see Castañeda, *Mexican Side of the Texan Revolution,* 103–104. For the de la Peña account, see Crisp, "The Little Book That Wasn't There: The Myth and Mystery of the de la Peña Diary," *Southwestern Historical Quarterly* 98, no. 2 (October 1994): 288–89. Although Dan Kilgore cites the Castañeda translation as the source of the Martínez Caro quotation on page 17 of *How Did Davy Die?* Kilgore actually provides a variant translation of the Spanish, the source of which I have not been able to identify. Kilgore or an associate may have translated this passage directly from the 1837 Mexico City edition of Martínez Caro's *Verdadera Idea de la Primera Campaña de Tejas y Sucesos Ocurridos después de la Acción de San Jacinto* and then inadvertently cited the standard published English translation as the source. This was a surprising discovery.

92. Groneman, *Defense of a Legend,* 60.

93. The "*pabellón*" issue and others were debated in a series of three articles in the *Alamo Journal* by Thomas Ricks Lindley, followed by three of my rebuttals. All of the articles have been collected online at the following site: http://www.tamu.edu/ccbn/dewitt/adp/archives/delapena/delapena1.html.

94. William C. Davis, "How Davy Probably *Didn't* Die," *Journal of the Alamo Battlefield Association* 2, no. 1 (Fall 1997): 26–28.

95. On September 28, 1836, the *Courier and New-York Enquirer* of New York City quoted the Dolson Letter from the *Detroit Free Press* by way of the *Rochester Daily Advertiser.* My thanks to Gregg Dimmick for this citation.

96. These same arguments, on both sides, are of course applicable to the other narrative of Crockett's death to emerge from the Mexican prisoner-of-war camp on Galveston Island—the one reported by the anonymous correspondent for the *New York Courier and Enquirer* and quoted by Kilgore on pages 19–21 of *How Did Davy Die?* It is very likely that the two reports of Crockett's death from the prisoner-of-war camp—this narrative and Dolson's—resulted from separate interviews with the same prisoner.

97. *Courier and New-York Enquirer* (New York City), September 28, 1836, quoting the Dolson Letter as reprinted in the *Rochester Daily Advertiser*. The Rochester editor believed that the informant was Almonte. Lind, "Death of David Crockett," 50–57. The web site containing a critical discussion of Lind's article, including Lind's rebuttal and my own response, is cited in note 69, above. Lind is the author of an epic poem of almost three hundred pages on the Battle of the Alamo, written in tightly rhymed classical verse. See Michael Lind, *The Alamo: An Epic* (Boston and New York: Houghton Mifflin Company, 1997).

98. Lord, *A Time to Stand,* 206; Perry, "Translator's Preface," in de la Peña, *With Santa Anna in Texas,* 1975 edition, xiv.

99. John H. Jenkins, *Basic Texas Books: An Annotated Bibliography of Selected Works for a Research Library,* revised edition (Austin: Texas State Historical Association, 1988), 100–101; Hutton, "Introduction," in Schoelwer, *Alamo Images,* 14; Paul Andrew Hutton, "A Tale of Two Alamos," *SMU Mustang* (Spring, 1986): 25; Hutton, "Introduction," in *A Narrative of the Life of David Crockett,* lv, note 44.

For a discussion of the causes of John Jenkins's confusion with respect to the publication date, see my article "The Little Book That Wasn't There," 280–82. After the 1994 appearance of this article, which established the accuracy of the 1955 first publication date of the de la Peña diary, Hutton, without explanation or citation, altered his texts in two subsequent reprintings of the works cited above to reflect the change from 1836 to 1955. See Paul Andrew Hutton, "The Alamo as Icon," in *The Texas Military Experience: From the Texas Revolution through World War II,* ed. Joseph G. Dawson III (College Station: Texas A&M University Press, 1995), 25; this is a revised version of the introduction to *Alamo Images.*

The change from 1836 to 1955 in note 44 on page lv of Hutton's introduction to Crockett's autobiography came in either the fourth or fifth printing of the Bison Book edition. The third printing still carried Hutton's original claim that "Lieutenant Colonel de la Peña's diary was first published in Mexico in 1836." By the fifth printing the statement had been changed to read: " Written in 1836, Lieutenant de la Peña's diary was first published in Mexico in 1955 by A. Frank de Sánchez." Hutton was still not stating the case accurately. While the diary was indeed written in 1836, what was published in Mexico City in 1955 was the memoir based on the diary. The diary itself has never been published. See Crisp, "Introduction," in de la Peña, *With Santa Anna in Texas*, rev. 1997 ed., xi–xxv.

100. See Crisp, "The Little Book That Wasn't There," 260–96; and Crisp, "Introduction," in *With Santa Anna in Texas*, rev. 1997 ed., xi–xxv.

101. See especially, in addition to Hutton's writings cited below, Hutton, "Davy Crockett: Still King of the Wild Frontier," 122–30, 244–48.

102. Dan Kilgore, review of *Crockett: A Bio-Bibliography*, by Richard Boyd Hauck, in the *Journal of the Early Republic* 4, no. 3 (Autumn 1984): 342–44.

103. Statement by Kilgore in the 1993 Huberman/Kilgore video interview.

104. Carrico, "CCSU Gets Kilgore Texas History Collection."

105. Interview with Thomas H. Kreneck, March 5, 2008. Dan Kilgore died on December 23, 1995. See Heines, "Prominent Local Historian and Accountant Kilgore Dies at 74."

106. Biffle, "Surrender? Davy's Fans Never Will."

107. Kent Biffle, "How Davy Died Still Stirs Debate," *Dallas Morning News*, November 24, 1985; Rick Smith, "Symposium Debunks Myths Surrounding the Alamo," *Dallas Times Herald*, November 17, 1985; Clifton H. Jones, "Foreword," in Schoelwer, *Alamo Images*, viii.

108. Smith, "Symposium Debunks Myths"; Jones, "Foreword," in Schoelwer, *Alamo Images*, xi; Biffle, "How Davy Died Still Stirs Debate."

109. Jones, "Foreword," in Schoelwer, *Alamo Images*, xii.

110. Smith, "Symposium Debunks Myths Surrounding the Alamo."

111. Hutton, "Introduction," in Schoelwer, *Alamo Images*, 3.

112. Kilgore, "Why Davy Didn't Die," 10. Hutton was also a contributor to the volume in which this article appeared; see Paul Andrew Hutton, "Davy Crockett: An Exposition on Hero Worship," in Lofaro and Cummings, *Crockett at Two Hundred*, 20–41.

113. Lofaro and Cummings, eds., *Crockett at Two Hundred*, xix.

114. Statement by Kilgore in the 1993 Huberman/Kilgore video interview.

115. David Pasztor, "Hero or Hoax? Historians Shoot Holes in Crockett's Musket-Toting Legend," *Dallas Times Herald*, August 16, 1986.

116. Ibid.

117. Ibid.

118. Ibid.

119. Wardlaw to Kilgore, May 2, 1977, Kilgore Collection.

120. Kilgore, "Why Davy Didn't Die," 10; *Handbook of Texas Online,* s.v. "Potter, Reuben Marmaduke" and "Zuber, William Physick."

121. *Handbook of Texas Online,* s.v. "Potter, Reuben Marmaduke."

122. Kilgore, "Why Davy Didn't Die," 10–11.

123. Ibid., 12–13.

124. Sam DeShong Ratcliffe, *Painting Texas History to 1900* (Austin: University of Texas Press, 1992), 21–23.

125. Kilgore, "Why Davy Didn't Die," 11–12. The detail of Crockett's final struggle as depicted in McArdle's *Dawn at the Alamo* illustrated the front of the dust jacket of *How Did Davy Die?*

126. Ratcliffe, *Painting Texas History,* xxii; *Handbook of Texas Online,* s.v. "DeShields, James Thomas."

127. For a more complete discussion of these iconic paintings and their profound influence on the Texan collective imagination (or "collective memory"), see James E. Crisp, "The Paintbrush and the Knife," *Sleuthing the Alamo: Davy Crockett's Last Stand and Other Mysteries of the Texas Revolution* (New York: Oxford University Press, 2004), 139–78; James E. Crisp, "An Incident in San Antonio: The Contested Iconology of Davy Crockett's Death at the Alamo," *Journal of the West* 40, no. 2 (Spring 2001): 67–77; and James E. Crisp, "Memory, Truth, and Pain: Myth and Censorship in the Celebration of Texas History," in *Lone Star Pasts: Memory and History in Texas,* ed. Gregg Cantrell and Elizabeth Hayes Turner (College Station: Texas A&M University Press, 2007), 75–94.

128. Kilgore, "Why Davy Didn't Die," 12.

129. Crisp, *Sleuthing the Alamo,* 171.

130. Kilgore, "Why Davy Didn't Die," 12.

131. Smith, "Symposium Debunks Myths Surrounding the Alamo" (first quotation); Hutton, "Introduction," in Schoelwer, *Alamo Images,* 13 (second and third quotations).

132. Henry Cabot Lodge and Theodore Roosevelt, *Hero Tales from American History* (New York: Century Company, 1895), 180.

133. See Crisp, *Sleuthing the Alamo,* 148–49.

134. See the nearly identical statements in Hutton, "Introduction," in Schoelwer, *Alamo Images,* 13, and Hutton, "Davy Crockett: An Exposition on Hero Worship," 31. When Hutton published a slightly abridged and revised version of his introduction to *Alamo Images* in 1995, this statement remained

intact, though he did alter the date of the first publication of the de la Peña diary from 1836 to 1955 to match Kilgore's conclusion on that matter. See Hutton, "Alamo as Icon," in 25. See also above, note 99.

135. Kilgore, "Why Davy Didn't Die," 7 (quotation), 16.

136. See above, notes 99 and 100.

137. Hutton, "Davy Crockett: An Exposition on Hero Worship," 28 (first quotation); Kilgore, "Why Davy Didn't Die," 17 (second quotation).

138. Jones, "Foreword," in Schoelwer, *Alamo Images*, x; Hutton, "Introduction," in Schoelwer, *Alamo Images*, 4 (quotation).

139. Hutton, "Introduction," in Schoelwer, *Alamo Images*, 6.

140. Ibid., 3.

141. Edward Tabor Linenthal, *Sacred Ground: Americans and Their Battlefields* (Urbana and Chicago: University of Illinois Press, 1991), 66.

142. C. W. Raines, "The Alamo Monument," *Quarterly of the Texas State Historical Association* 6, no. 4 (April 1903): 305.

143. Hutton, "Introduction," in Schoelwer, *Alamo Images*, 6.

144. See R. M. Potter, "The Texas Revolution: Distinguished Mexicans Who Took Part in the Revolution of Texas, with Glances at Its Early Events," *Magazine of American History* 2, no. 10 (October 1878): 577–603.

145. Kilgore, "Why Davy Didn't Die," 10 (first quotation), 11 (second quotation).

146. Ibid., 11.

147. See Joseph Campbell (with Bill Moyers), *The Power of Myth* (New York: Doubleday, 1988).

148. Hutton, "Introduction," in Schoelwer, *Alamo Images*, 4 (first and second quotations), 6 (third quotation).

149. Emily Fourmy Cutrer, "'The Hardy, Stalwart Sons of Texas': Art and Mythology at the Capitol," *Southwestern Historical Quarterly* 92, no. 2 (October 1988): 307–308.

150. See Cecilia Elizabeth O'Leary, "Blood Brotherhood: The Racialization of Patriotism," in *Bonds of Affection: Americans Define Their Patriotism*, ed. John Bodnar (Princeton, N.J.: Princeton University Press, 1996), 53–81.

151. David W. Blight, *Race and Reunion: The Civil War in American Memory* (Cambridge: Harvard University Press, 2001).

152. David Montejano, *Anglos and Mexicans in the Making of Texas, 1836–1986* (Austin: University of Texas Press, 1987), 223–24.

153. Ironically, Juan Seguín, the Tejano patriot turned "traitor" who returned to Texas after the war between Mexico and the United States to become once more a respected citizen of San Antonio, was one of the chief

historical consultants of Reuben M. Potter, Henry McArdle's principal advisor in the creation of *Dawn at the Alamo.* Potter's unbiased opinion with regard to Seguín speaks to the character of both men:

> Colonel Seguin served gallantly as a Captain under General Houston at San Jacinto, and subsequently commanded a regiment. His zealous adherence to the cause of Texas throughout the campaign of 1836, and for some years after, is undoubted; and his subsequent defection from that cause may be palliated by the popular harshness, endangering life, to which he became subject, and which in a manner drove him to a step of which he evidently repented. I have no reason to doubt the candor and correctness of anything which he related in matters whereon I have cited his authority. He had no motive to misrepresent anything which was not personal to himself, nor did he seem to color unduly what was. A man may be a correct narrator in spite of political errors.

See Reuben M. Potter, "The Fall of the Alamo," *Magazine of American History* 2, no. 1 (January 1878): note 5. Accessed July 16, 1998: http://flash.net/~alam03/archives/potter/potter01.htm.

154. Montejano, *Anglos and Mexicans,* 220 (first quotation), 224 (second quotation).

155. Holly Beachley Brear, *Inherit the Alamo: Myth and Ritual at an American Shrine* (Austin: University of Texas Press, 1995), 23–63; Richard R. Flores, "Memory-Place, Meaning, and the Alamo," *American Literary History* 10, no. 3 (Fall 1998): 433, 443. In fairness to the present caretakers of the Alamo, it should be noted that several important changes, both substantive and symbolic, have been made at the site since Brear and Flores conducted the bulk of their fieldwork. For example, a Mexican national flag has been added to those mounted in the Hall of Honor representing the native countries of the defenders, and the filmstrip that Flores found particularly objectionable was replaced in 1997 by a video with a less "binary" (and more historically accurate) presentation of the conflict.

156. Richard R. Flores, *Remembering the Alamo: Memory, Modernity, and the Master Symbol* (Austin: University of Texas Press, 2002), xiii.

157. Crisp, *Sleuthing the Alamo,* 152 (from a conversation with Andrés Tijerina).

158. Private conversation with the author; confirmed August 8, 2009. My informant wishes to remain anonymous.

159. Linenthal, *Sacred Ground,* 71–72.

160. Joe B. Frantz to Frank Wardlaw, April 27, 1978, A&M Press Back Files. The Clara Driscoll Scholarship for Research in Texas History was established at the University of Texas at Austin in 1943 with a gift from the Daughters of the Republic of Texas. See H. Bailey Carroll, "Texas Collection," *Southwestern Historical Quarterly* 47, no. 2 (October 1943): 177.

161. Joe B. Frantz to Frank Wardlaw, April 27, 1978, A&M Press Back Files.

162. W. Fitzhugh Brundage, "Introduction: No Deed but Memory," in *Where These Memories Grow: History, Memory, and Southern Identity,* ed. W. Fitzhugh Brundage (Chapel Hill and London: UNC Press, 2000), 13.

163. Ibid., 3–4.

164. Biffle, "How Davy Died Still Stirs Debate."

165. Brundage, ""Introduction" in *Where These Memories Grow,* 13.

166. Groneman, *Defense of a Legend,* 41.

167. Flores, *Remembering the Alamo,* 147–48.

168. Ibid., 151.

169. The only known direct reference by Kilgore to the racial comments in his mail is his tongue-in-cheek private comment to Frank Wardlaw that only those who could "understand the plot to defame white American heroes" would know the real reasons for Wardlaw's retirement from the Texas A&M Press in 1978. (See above, note 61). However, in the late 1980s, Kilgore made his scrapbook of letters available to cultural historian Edward Tabor Linenthal, who was including a chapter on the Alamo in his book *Sacred Ground: Americans and Their Battlefields.* Although Linenthal did not address the details of the Crockett controversy in his text, in a lengthy footnote he discussed some of the racially tinged mail Dan had received. This is the only published reference to the racial material received by Kilgore that I found before publishing my own commentary on it in *Sleuthing the Alamo* (pages 139–50). See Linenthal, *Sacred Ground,* 84–85, note 51.

170. Montejano, *Anglos and Mexicans,* 285, 289.

171. Kreneck, "Dan Kilgore: 'Demon Collector,'" 163–64; royalty statements, Kilgore Collection. Dan's two biggest years of royalties from *How Did Davy Die?* were 1978 ($449.22) and 1986 ($195.80). In Dan's handwriting on an adding machine slip with the royalty statements is the notation "Lifetime Royalties—$1,230.61."

172. George Ward to Dan Kilgore, June 28, 1993, Kilgore Collection.

173. Dan Kilgore to George Ward, July 9, 1993, Kilgore Collection.

174. Bill Groneman, "The Diary of José Enrique de la Peña," typescript in Kilgore Collection.

175. Dan Kilgore to George Ward, July 9, 1993, Kilgore Collection.

176. "Southwestern Collection," *Southwestern Historical Quarterly* 97, no. 4 (April 1994): 675.

177. James E. Crisp, "Sam Houston's Speechwriters: The Grad Student, the Teenager, the Editors, and the Historians," *Southwestern Historical Quarterly* 97, no. 2 (October 1993): 202–37.

178. See Crisp, "The Little Book That Wasn't There," 260–96.

179. Jan Reid, "Davy Crock?" *Texas Monthly* (May 1995); Huberman, *The De la Peña Diary.*

180. Biffle, "Surrender? Davy's Fans Never Will"; Hutton, "Davy Crockett: An Exposition on Hero Worship," 20–41. Hutton describes both his own and Kilgore's hate mail in this essay, but does not mention any racial content.

181. For an expanded version of the Italian presentation, see Crisp, "An Incident in San Antonio," 67–77.

182. For my debates with Lindley, see above, note 93. See also William Groneman, "The Controversial Alleged Account of José Enrique de la Peña," *Military History of the West* 25, no. 2 (Fall 1995): 129–42; James E. Crisp, "A Reply: When Revision Becomes Obsession: Bill Groneman and the de la Peña Diary," *Military History of the West* 25, no. 2 (Fall 1995): 143–55; William Groneman, "A Rejoinder: Publish Rather than Perish—Regardless," *Military History of the West* 25, no. 2 (Fall 1995): 157–65; James E. Crisp, "Truth, Confusion, and the de la Peña Controversy: A Final Reply," *Military History of the West* 26, no. 1 (Spring 1996): 99–104; William Groneman, "A Last Final Reply: or, How I Learned to Stop Worrying and Love Jim Crisp," *Military History of the West* 26, no. 1 (Spring 1996): 105–106.